UNIVERSAL SPIRIT

*The Seasons
of the*
Christian Year
*in the
Company of*
Northrop
Frye

DON COLLETT

UNIVERSAL SPIRIT

*The Seasons
of the
Christian Year
in the
Company of*
**Northrop
Frye**

WOOD LAKE

Editor: Mike Schwartzentruber
Proofreader: Pattie Bender
Design: Robert MacDonald

Library and Archives Canada Cataloguing in Publication
Title: Universal spirit : the seasons of the Christian year in the company of
Northrop Frye / Don Collett.
Names: Collett, Don, 1953- author.
Description: Includes bibliographical references.
Identifiers: Canadiana (print) 20190048409 | Canadiana (ebook) 20190048476 |
ISBN 9781773430348 (softcover) | ISBN 9781773431499 (HTML)
Subjects: LCSH: Church year. | LCSH: Spirituality. | LCSH: Frye, Northrop,
Criticism and interpretation.
Classification: LCC BV30 .C65 2019 | DDC 263/.9–dc23

Unless otherwise indicated, all scripture quotations are taken from the *Revised
English Bible*, copyright © Cambridge University Press and Oxford University
Press 1989. All rights reserved. Scripture quotations marked (JB) are from the
Jerusalem Bible copyright © 1966, 1967, 1968 Darton, Longman, and Todd LTD
and Doubleday and Co. Inc. All rights reserved. Scripture quotations marked
(KJV) are from the *King James Version*, public domain.

ISBN 978-1-77343-034-8

Published by Wood Lake Publishing Inc.
485 Beaver Lake Road, Kelowna, BC, Canada, V4V 1S5
www.woodlake.com | 250.766.2778

Wood Lake Publishing acknowledges the financial support of the Government of
Canada. Wood Lake Publishing acknowledges the financial support of the
Province of British Columbia through the Book Publishing Tax Credit.

Wood Lake Publishing would like to acknowledge that we operate in the unceded
territory of the Syilx/Okanagan People, and we work to support reconciliation and
challenge the legacies of colonialism. The Syilx/Okanagan territory is a diverse
and beautiful landscape of deserts and lakes, alpine forests and endangered
grasslands. We honour the ancestral stewardship of the Sylix/Okanagan People.

Printed in Canada.
Printing 10 9 8 7 6 5 4 3 2 1

CONTENTS

FOR SANDRA SEVERS

MY LIFE WITH NORRIE

Christianity [is] a truly ideal foolishness...
a childlike trust and hope for the human condition
that left open the realm of mystery ...

Or we might better say that Christianity took
creature consciousness – the thing [we] most
wanted to deny – and made it
the very *condition for* [our] cosmic heroism.
– Ernest Becker, *The Denial of Death*[1]

To HIS FRIENDS HE WAS NORRIE. During the first year of my seminary training at Emmanuel College, one of my professors – who was a friend of Northrop Frye (or who pretended to be) – would now and then refer to him as Norrie. Of course, we all knew who he meant. In the 1980s, Northrop Frye's picture or bust or name could be seen everywhere on the Victoria University campus, which was part of the University of Toronto campus. He was an august and holy presence at high table at lunch and at the various mundane meetings he had to attend as chancellor. More often, one might pass him by chance on the way to class.

One time I passed him and, at the same time, I said to myself out loud, "Norrie, eh?" We happened to be crossing paths under an arch between residences. Unbeknownst to me, the space was reverberant and alive with echoes. He heard me. He stopped, turned in my direction, and glared. I was horrified. But I just carried on as if nothing happened. I lived with the shame for years.

When his book *The Great Code* was published and *Maclean's* magazine did an article on him, I passed him again while he was being photographed for the article. He was apologizing to the photographer for the missing button on his worn tweed sports jacket.

In 1981, when I graduated from Emmanuel College to become a minister in The United Church of Canada, Frye laid his hands over mine and admitted me to the degree Master of Divinity. Later that day, he paid me the highest compliment. He said that my valedictorian address to the graduating class was the best he had ever heard. George Ignatieff, then chancellor of the University of Toronto, told me that at the tea following convocation. I have always wondered what I said that impressed him so much. And now I have no idea what I said in that speech at all.

Such were the faint glimmers of my future partnership with Northrop Frye. They showed again when he gave a lecture to the alumni of Emmanuel College the year after I graduated. I was intrigued, but quite oblivious to what was said. I was more impressed by how embarrassing my colleagues' questions were afterward. They had no idea what he was talking about either, but hadn't the good sense to shut up. Later, I realized that he was delivering excerpts from the introduction to *The Great Code*.

I remember the day he died. I was on my way south from Calgary to Lethbridge in southern Alberta, to attend a meeting of my local presbytery. I heard the news on CBC (Canadian Broadcasting Corporation) radio. I did not cry, but I was deeply saddened. I wondered how empty the Victoria University campus must have seemed on that day and on those that followed, his giant intellectual presence having passed from the place forever. His painting, his bust, and the building which bore his name now hollow representations of the great and good person he was.

I announced Frye's death to the meeting when I arrived and we spent a few moments sharing our personal stories of him. I cannot remember any other instance of the death of a single person affecting a large United Church meeting like that. Everyone knew he was our greatest. We had a sense that a legend had passed, perhaps the last giant left in the land in the waning years of mainline Protestantism in Canada. He was the very best our tradition had produced and perhaps would ever produce.

* * *

When I was an active minister in The United Church of Canada, I lived two distinct but intertwined lives: the life of a churchman with its apparent accoutrements of religious insight, moral straightness, and wise discernment; and the life of a spouse, parent, citizen, and administrator, not necessarily in that order. The one life constrained me mostly to the expectations of others. The other life, in contrast, appeared like any other middle-class existence, full of welcome ordinariness.

Perhaps my life was not so singular in its duality. In some ways, this kind of duality and its attempted resolution is the fate of all spiritual people. For us there is, as John the evangelist said, a way of being in the world, but not of it. My particularity as a minister lay in leadership, and in the regular Sunday morning ritual of worship where, at best, I bridged my worlds and the worlds of my people through my words. The great theologian Walter Brueggemann called my kind "a poet of the gospel," one who speaks honestly about the incongruity, and buoyantly about the alternatives.[2] This was my fervent hope.

For most of his 50-odd years as a university teacher, Frye lived these two lives also. He too was a minister in The United Church of Canada, but rarely inhabited a pulpit in the usual way. His pulpit was his classroom, but his discipline, in contrast to my own, was to witness without preaching, to testify but never confess. He felt it highly unethical to share his faith stance with his students. Nevertheless, the breadth of his faith shone through in his passion as a teacher and a critic. He considered his witness to be the articulation of form to culture. Christianity and its texts were inextricably tied into that culture. In the tradition of the United Church, to find the connection between Christian faith and culture is possibly the highest calling and in some ways fits the larger purpose of the denomination itself.

To my knowledge, Frye became a public apologist for the faith only in the last years of his life. His two big books on the Bible – *The Great Code* and *Words with Power* – showed not a hint of what was to come in the year before his death: a slender volume called *The Double Vision: Language and Meaning in Religion*. In *The Double Vision*, he let the veil down. In this last book, those of us who admired him and wondered about his theology could finally see the believer in all his penetrating insight and wisdom.

It wasn't enough for me, however. It just whetted my appetite. I wanted more. Only with the publication of his other unpublished works on religion in 2000, and later his notebooks, was I able to get food for a real feast. They provide a cornucopia for the intelligent person of the spirit, not in the articles, sermons, and prayers themselves usually, but in the little bits he throws to us as asides.

Here is an example. At a memorial service for students who died during the previous term during the time he was principal of Victoria College in January 1963, he said this prayer. It seems a timeless response to the death of the young.

Through all the cruelty of nature and the malice of man, we hear the exultant song of the life that knows no death: the hymns of thy angels sound in the ruins of our cities: thy eternal purpose shapes to thy will all the destruction that our folly can invent or our fury unloose.[3]

These are inspired words from a person deeply in love with the world and its people. I found myself returning to these words when, as a minister, I helped my own people deal with the calamity of 9/11, the suicides that intruded on my own life during that time, and the tsunami of Boxing Day 2004. Thereafter, I returned to those words and many other passages in the writing he left behind as I listened to the pain of my clients in my practice as a psychotherapist. Here is vision among the smoke and the ashes of human life on this planet.

* * *

In a strange way, through the process of going back to him over and over like this, Northrop Frye and I became partners in the faith. I found it a rare experience as a student of spirituality to read a theologian whose breadth of reading is so large that the Bible is but a piece of the whole, and for whom the Bible provides a lens through which the whole is seen. Frye conceived of a world beyond the normal confines of Christian doctrine and theology and then, latterly, found a way for Christian doctrine and theology to provide the hope this world needs. As I increasingly addressed myself to people for whom the Bible is not a lens, this was a priceless gift, for I could have conversations that seemed wholly secular and be very clear inside myself that this was also the vocabulary of faith.

Frye had a passion for this kind of conversation and it is a conversation I propose to further with this book. I want it to be a discussion of the human from a spiritual if not restrictively Christian point of view. I no longer find the confines of the church nor the Christian tradition to be the boundary around which such conversations may happen. Northrop Frye never did.

Frye's diligence in maintaining contact with contemporary culture so that he could communicate with his students is invaluable to the contemporary spiritual thinker today, as is his larger role as cultural critic. While Frye's writing concerning biblical texts is sometimes obscure, every theological concept he writes about has a touchstone not only in scripture and tradition, but also in the real world of human experience. Scripture, tradition, and real-world experience were, for Frye, in a continual conversation, and it was, and remains, the critic's job to bring them together in some coherent way.

I cannot help wondering whether Frye's dedication to his students and to the contemporary world in which they lived and breathed and had their being – a "contemporary" world in which people wrestled with the same spiritual struggles as we do today – derived from the existential crises he experienced himself as a student, and from the necessity he might have felt to find a religious or spiritual way to address the needs that arose from them: the misbegotten venture into professional ministry for which he was completely ill-suited; the early struggle to find nurture and success in academia; his relationship with Helen Kemp, who would become his wife, but not before two abortions and many physical separations; the cruel irony of their childlessness after marriage and the collective sorrow of this absence that weighed so heavily upon them. The untold grief from these struggles and losses must have allowed a lasting sympathy for all who struggle and suffer.

For a person like me, a seeker who attempts to connect the larger world with the spiritual world, Frye's insights have been a lifeline. In the years after 9/11 it seemed as though something broke loose in spiritual consciousness. It is almost as if an opportunity opened up in the wake of that unprecedented evil. People became more curious about spirituality not confined so much to the doctrine of any particular faith tradition. A sense of the deeper purpose of the human started coming to the fore, helping people live their lives with an unconfined hope. As it happened, the beginning of this spiritual renaissance coincided with my reading and re-reading of Frye on spiritual matters. In him I found a vision that filled out my own vision and my own commitment to a wider spiritual life.

This is partly because the biblical texts, always intriguing to Frye, not only form the basis of mainline Protestant faith in general and United Church theology in particular, they have the potential to open up the

spiritual life to all people. What strikes one when reading Frye's central texts is how devoid of religious language they are. He returns repeatedly to Hebrews 11:1
in which the Pauline writer speaks of faith as, "the
assurance of things hoped for, the conviction of things
unseen." Frye translates the same line, helpfully, as
"Faith is the realization of human hopes, the dialectic
of the invisible."[4] In his own translation, Frye expresses
his fundamental belief about how faith arises in the
human. For him, faith develops over time as human
hopes approach some kind of fulfillment. This end is
not accidental nor inevitable. It comes as a result of an
internal struggle or dialogue between contending voices
in which a hopeful outcome is foreshadowed or suggested. We get a flavour of Frye's meaning when we
hear Desmond Tutu say that he is not an optimist but
a prisoner of hope.[5] Here, for Tutu and for Frye, hope
is something drawn forth from an unseen force that
cannot be refused. Perhaps this is as close as we can
come to describing faith as a human phenomenon.

Frye also gives singular attention to Paul's poem on
love in 1 Corinthians 13:1–13 and goes so far as to say
that if there is any certainty in spiritual matters, we can
be sure that the language of love is the language that is
spoken by God.[6] This, even though the Pauline poem
makes no explicit reference to God at all! How reassur-
ing, then, that the language of God can be spoken by all
people.

* * *

I did not begin reading Northrop Frye's theology thinking that he would be my visionary angel on spiritual matters; I just kept going back to him when, as a preacher, I was stuck. As I struggled, I discovered new riches in myself and in him. That is what, in the widest sense, a true prophet does. That is what a wise teacher does and is.

What follows is a spiritual year in the company of Northrop Frye, a year that now borders on 25 years for me. As such, this is not a systematic treatment of Frye's thought; it is the work of a struggling seeker trying to make sense of the seasons of the church year and their different nuances. The seasons of the church year – Advent through Pentecost – may seem arcane to some, and an odd choice for organizing this material, but I take the view that Christianity's way of organizing the year into seasons is actually quite helpful as a way to draw forth insights into what I will call the "universal spirit" – spiritual truths that may be applied in the course of a person's everyday life. There is a comprehensive way of living that both Frye and I see flowing from the biblical tradition unconstrained by the weight of orthodox theology. Just as Michelangelo said he found Moses in a block of Carrera marble, so in biblical myth we find a universality that provides meaning in the course of human life and action. So the seasons of the church year, and the biblical texts associated with them, still seem a vastly rich and fertile place from which to survey the human landscape and to find the universal spirit's place within it.

At times in what follows, Frye provides the centre for my meditations; at others he provides a jumping off point. I think of these pieces as a survey of my spiritual passion with the aid, at times, of the spiritual passion of another kindred spirit – similar to how jazz musicians riff off one another in performance. It is my hope that these pieces will appeal to people who desire to make sense of some key spiritual concepts and topics, and who are curious about the way both intersect with the challenging events of our times.

As I review what I've written here, there are places where I have a sense that Frye is in the text, but I am not sure where. For example, I was sure Frye taught me that the story of Pentecost is the reversal of the Babel myth, but I could no longer remember where that insight lay in his writings until my editor pointed to the spot in Frye's book *The Great Code*.[7] As a result, the reader may find phrases or ideas that belong to Frye but that are unacknowledged. My only excuse is that his language seems to have entered my consciousness so that at times I wonder where he leaves off and where I begin. I can honestly say about him what he said about his own mentor and muse William Blake: "Everything I learned, I learned from him." I am happy to attribute this whole book to him, for his passion feels so very close to my own. Indeed, his passion seems very close to the passion of my spiritual tradition or what it *should* be. My mistakes may be everywhere in evidence, but they are mine and mine alone.

Above all, this book is dedicated to the memory of Northrop Frye and to his faithful dedication to spiritual truth in secular culture. My hope is that through his effort and mine, others will find solace and vision. As slight as my understanding may be, I enthusiastically share it with you now.

NOTES

1. Ernest Becker, *The Denial of Death* (New York: The Free Press, 1973), 204, 160.
2. Walter Brueggemann, *Finally Comes the Poet: Daring Speech for Proclamation* (Minneapolis: Fortress Press, 1989), 17.
3. Northrop Frye, *The Collected Works of Northrop Frye: Northrop Frye on Religion*, eds. Alvin A. Lee and Jean O'Grady, vol. 4 (Toronto: University of Toronto Press, 1991), 278.
4. Ibid., 8.
5. Piers Morgan, *Tonight*, on CNN, 26 April 2011, as recalled by David Frost. Frost says to Tutu, "I always think of you as an optimist." Tutu stops him and says, "I'm not an optimist, I'm a prisoner of hope."
6. Northrop Frye, *The Double Vision: Language and Meaning in Religion* (Toronto: University of Toronto Press, 1991), 21.
7. Northrop Frye, *The Great Code: The Bible and Literature* (New York: Harcourt Brace Jovanovich Publishers, 1981), 158.

ADVENT

[O]ur ancestors in the forest watching the sun grow fainter
until it was a cold weak light...chose the shortest day of
the year to defy almost triumphant darkness.
We have learned that we do not need to worry about the
sun, and there isn't a monster big enough to swallow it.
— Northrop Frye, *Collected Works*[1]

FOR NORTHROP FRYE, A SPIR-
ITUAL TRUTH is that which seeks to show what a wider
human freedom actually looks like.[2] These spiritual truths,
as he explains in his book *The Double Vision*, are en-
cased in the language of metaphor and myth. We cannot know what is spiritually true except as we strain to
describe how one thing is like another, or by using
figurative narratives or myths in which human experience is episodically described and brought to some end.
It is only in the liminal space we enter in metaphor and
in myth that truths of the spiritual kind can be encountered and explored.

For Frye, some narratives are better at revealing
spiritual truths than others. The Bible is a collection of

texts that has endured the test of time and that has reliably revealed the spiritual concerns of humans in its narrative. The New Testament conveys "a vision of the spiritual life that continues to transform and expand our own," Frye says.[3] In other words, the New Testament and the other texts of the Christian Bible contain myths to live *by* as well as *in*.[4] It is in this lifestyle that, for Frye, freedom of the spiritual kind resides.

The Christian portion of the Bible has become central to the spiritual experience in the West, but it is by no means the only source concerning truths of a spiritual kind. For me and for most people raised in the Christian tradition, it just happens to be the most familiar narrative and therefore the most helpful.

The latter quarter of the Bible is concerned about what happens when Jesus comes into the world, but if you are not concerned about Jesus that does not mean it is vacant of spiritual truth; one simply has to be more discerning. For the purposes of this book, we are concerned about how parts of the Christian tradition may inform wider spiritual concerns. As we will see, there are many.

Apart from the message about what happens to Jesus and doctrinal concerns about his lordship, for Frye, the bottom line is that the language of love revealed in the Bible is the closest we get to the language God speaks.

It is therefore the kind of language to which we may give attention to our benefit, beginning with the time of Advent.

OF PREPARATION AND PROPHECY

The Christian year begins with the four weeks before Christmas Day. The season is called Advent or Coming. Advent is one of the two principal times in the church year (the other being Lent), when we are invited to review our lives and to repent of misdeeds or actions that have hurt others or ourselves. It is a time of preparation and reflection in anticipation of a new kind of blessing.

In their practical souls, most mainline Protestant Christians have never grasped the need for penitence over an extended period. A little prayer at the beginning of worship now and then should, in their view, suffice. And as soon as the air gets chilly and the snow starts to fly, they want to cart out the Christmas carols. For those who have cast off or at least put some distance between the traditional Christian catechism and their own spiritual lives, the need for penance seems arcane, if not actually harmful and counterproductive. What, if anything, is there to gain from it?

As if to underline this aversion, the Advent readings in the Bible are rife with stories of apocalypse and John the baptizer, both, at first glance, less than exciting in the popular imagination. Apocalypse – while it mirrors what seems to be the inevitable movement of nature at the hands of humanity in our time – feels defeatist to read, and self-immolating. John the baptizer is the one you see in Old Masters paintings, dressed in unusual clothing, looking like he needs a good bath and a hot meal. Generally, in these paintings, John points away from himself to the blessed countenance of Jesus some distance away on the other side of the painting. That is because the gospels show us someone with little to say except "Repent!" This leads us to wonder whether the man has any emotional core at all. Think Friedrich Nietzsche in Goth dress. Tell us why, we say, besides the fact that we are bad or misguided people.

Almost certainly Jesus was John's disciple and the controversy about who really was messiah, Jesus or John, is behind this sketchy picture of a great personage. The gospels tell us that everyone flocked to John from Jerusalem, Judea, and the Jordan Valley to be baptized by him – including, according to Luke, his second cousin Jesus bar Joseph. *Everyone* came: rich and poor, powerful and weak, religious and wayward. If a peasant like John attracted the entire Jewish population to his ritual of baptism, and if the authorities thought his message dangerous enough to cut off his head, which they did, he must have had a little more depth.

In fact, it may be that much of Jesus' evangelical message comes from John. Even more importantly, John the baptizer may have been the first person to truly understand and preach the power of sacrament. He believed that humans could engage in an outward activity that would have a profound and transformative inner effect. He understood the notion that an action on the body could change the inner workings of the soul. Jesus, who understood the power of sacrament and invented his own at the Last Supper or Eucharist or Communion, may have appropriated this notion from John. Maybe John the baptizer is someone we need to reckon with, if not as those who are Christ-focused then as those who remain concerned about how to be more human in this world.

Pity the preacher, however. Four weeks of constructing something interesting around the gospel's portrayal of John and portents of the end of the world, while their congregants are chomping at the bit for Christmas carols. By Christmas Eve, things can get a bit testy. Happy are we who are liberated from this problem.

But let us turn back to this person, strange as he may be. For the sun is in decline, the nights lengthen, and we have, even as 21st-century people, a sense in our very core that there is cause for worry.

THE BAPTIZER AS FOOL

As the gospels paint him, John the baptizer was a winter kind of guy. He was as winsome as a winter storm. He wore scratchy camel hair. He ate a tasty combination of grasshoppers and wild honey. He called people names like "snake's children." He threatened that some people were chaff and others grain, and said that fire awaited the chaff. Best leave him off the list for your next dinner party. Remember, of course, this is early Christian propaganda.

In literary terms, however, he seems a bit of a fool, in the best sense of the word. In a wonderful piece on Shakespeare's *King Lear* contained in *Northrop Frye on*

Shakespeare, Frye writes of the intersection between the fool and the prophet in the character of the pre-Christian Lear. In a way, the readings in Advent invite us into the pre-Christian realm too.

For Frye, Shakespeare's fools are those who will not live according to the conditions of the lower or savage nature of the world, where people plot to kill, abuse others, and poke other people's eyes out. The fool is one who makes their home in a higher world, which the lower world disparages.[5] Lear learns this lesson the hard way. He begins with a sense of his own privilege, his entitlement, and then by giving it all away to the children of his first unhappy marriage and by banning the child of his beloved second marriage, he brings himself, almost by accident, into the land of the foolish. It is a descent in one sense, and an ascent in another. The main thing to note is that as the play proceeds Lear begins to understand the larger purpose of the human amongst humans. He comes to make his home in the world where love is the highest value. He is tossed out of doors onto a heath and into a howling storm where he encounters the elements in all their fury. Suddenly his attention is drawn to a homeless person. It is after this scene, his descent and his ascent, that Lear begins to notice the people around him in a new way.

Paul McCartney had a sense of this dual realm when he wrote the song "Fool on the Hill," in which the fool "sees the sun going down and the eyes in his head see the world spinning round ..."

Nobody, sings McCartney, wants to know this person because, well, he's just a fool. But when someone is passionate about a higher, more loving realm and lives in denial of the comfort of ordinary humans, people seem to pay attention, at least for a little while.

And so it was with this strange man, John the baptizer. His best message, unfettered from the propaganda, is pretty straightforward: "Pause and take an inventory! Pause and take stock! The language of love has more to tell you than you think. Pause. Once you have begun to listen not to the monkey-thoughts of the self-condemning narrative in your head but to the blessing you are to the world, then you may be ready for something better. Then you can get ready for something new to happen. For goodness sake, prepare for that way!"

BIBLICAL NARRATIVE AS PARADE

Here is another way to look at the message of John the baptizer. There is a voice in the wilderness calling to us: "Prepare a highway for something new to happen, something refreshing to enter your hearts. Make it straight. Make the valleys of your lives flat – don't dwell in them anymore. Make the obstacles in your lives, the mountains, low. Let there be no more winding, no more rough places, just a straight, smooth parade toward the good, toward the better."

One of the ways to look at the Bible and at the characters in it, and even at the larger narrative of the Bible, is as a kind of procession or parade. A procession has an importance all its own. Something special is happening. Even if people in a parade aren't important, a parade or procession *makes* them important. We process at graduations. We process at funerals and at weddings. We process at protest marches against pipelines. When something important is taking place, or we *want* it to be important, you can be sure there will be a procession in there somewhere. It is a strange, singular kind of human activity, which distinguishes us from other animals.

As a child, a parade was nearly as exciting for me as Christmas morning. This was because my family lived along the Stampede parade route in Calgary, Alberta. While everyone else had to get up at the screech of dawn to find a place, my family could have a casual breakfast and find a place along the boulevard.

Sitting on our lawn chairs, the then-famous – at least famous to me – would pass by just a few yards in front of us: Bing Crosby, Bob Hope, the Lone Ranger, even The Three Stooges. The most memorable famous person, though, was Robert Fitzgerald Kennedy, who passed by in 1966, two years before an assassin's bullet claimed him in the middle of his run toward the presidency of the United States.

These famous people were always in the middle of the procession, of course. There were bands and floats and clowns before them to get us ready, and bands and floats and clowns after them to ease us back into real life again.

The parade or procession is a practice deeply rooted in the Jewish and Christian traditions. The people of Israel processed out of Egypt into the wilderness. When they finally found their way back, they processed into the promised land. Later, the people of Israel were led away in a procession to exile in Babylon. Then, after a generation or two, they processed back. In the whole Bible, the parade also has an implicitly inward movement; the procession always represents a journey of the human spirit and, in the New Testament, it is explicitly so.

In the New Testament, the writers reach back to Hebrew tradition, reach back to those parades, reach back for the movement between slavery and freedom, bondage and redemption. Most important, the gospels reach back to those who were prophets, and to their message, and invite us to listen to them again.

So this particular tradition invites us to be in a kind of parade with our brothers and sisters, our mothers and fathers, and with our children – also from slavery to freedom, from bondage to redemption – during the time before Christmas called Advent.

It is important to note that our highway is not ours alone; we process with others, even with those who came before us. In this way we are not alone in our endeavour to free ourselves, but accompanied. I believe this is what all people want: company. As the solstice nears and anxiety about losing the sun begins to grow, think about your hopes and dreams, about your faith and your best intentions. Leave your failures and your frustrations behind, your pain and your struggle. Advent reminds us of promise. We embrace the prophetic – that procession from our lower nature to a higher one, as Frye would say. And, to paraphrase the great hymn "From the Slave Pens of the Delta" by Herbert O'Driscoll, we find our freedom and we discover new worlds for ourselves in which to live and move and have our being.[6]

Frye reminds us that it is into a prophetic vision such as this that Lear stumbles as he encounters the rejection of his daughters and the heath and the sorry creatures on it, even as the base elements of the earth pummel and torment him.[7] It is a prophetic vision we are called to experience too during Advent, as in our parade together we proceed toward the solstice. The foolish and prophetic John the baptizer may get us there.

But how different this is from what we practice in December, when pausing is the last thing we do! Typically, December is the busiest time of year! Retailers count on it. We do not slow down or stop to listen. Instead we get busy. We distract ourselves.

I heard John Ralston Saul say once that we have lost touch with the rhythm of our bodies, at least as they were configured in much earlier times. In previous eras, summer was a time of high activity because of the warmth and the relative ease with which life could be lived. Winter for our ancestors was a time of hardship and of slowing down, and therefore of contemplation, of reflecting on what had passed. It was a time when we recharged our batteries, painted our pictures, wrote our poetry and composed our songs. It was a sabbatical, just like God's mythical sabbatical after six busy days of making the world.

Frye reminds us that in the pre-Christian world, as the winter solstice approached, the shortest day, a sort of panic set in. It was so dark people were afraid they might lose the sun altogether. The panic inspired raging bonfires, lights, feasting, and the exchange of presents. Apparently, it was all about declaring loyalty to the sun so that it wouldn't leave! As Frye has noted, the modern equivalent of that ancient panic is our worry about how many shopping days are left before Christmas. In other words, that panic still resides deep within us and we are ripe for the prophetic message, its call, its challenge and, ultimately, its parade toward hope.[8]

DELVING DEEPER

Let's take a look at the merits of John's message. It was not based on beating ourselves up over our mistakes on the one hand, nor on a kind of blind optimism on the other – that if we just wait, good will come in the end. John believed that messiah, or truly embodied hope, would come only if we engaged in a kind of self-reflection. The water of his sacrament represented a fresh start. It was as if he was saying, "Wash away that which holds you back. Get on the highway forward toward something better."

So many defining moments in history have been preceded by a time of reflection, a time of taking stock, and we all need the opportunity to do this. Generals, as they consider the field of battle, need to assess the situation realistically, systematically, and critically. In times of crisis, especially, political leaders need to keep their heads and think of the larger picture. On the train trip to a battlefield-turned-graveyard, Abraham Lincoln – another person first considered a fool and later a prophet – jotted down a five-minute dedication speech called The Gettysburg Address and changed the way the Constitution of the United States would be viewed forever after. For the next 100 years and more, the American nation would struggle with the meaning of the word equality. Just a little looking out the window during the train trip and some jotting was all it took.

Perhaps this seems like a grand event far beyond what we will ever encounter, and maybe it is, but that's not the point. The point is our need to take stock, to take time to discern, to pay attention. That is what the time of the waning of the sun in our year is all about. And that is what John's message is all about.

I have noticed an upsurge in troubled people in my therapy practice since the election of Donald Trump, and I have noticed in myself a reluctance to listen to any news about him or his policies. But perhaps I should resist my resistance. Maybe we can take a page from the vibrant community of comedians who seem actually inspired by this turn of events. How can we be our best, how can we use our gifts to counter what seems to be a move toward the inhuman and the intolerant in the here and now?

On the 100th anniversary of the Nobel Prize, 100 Nobel laureates – including the Dalai Lama, Mikhail Gorbachev, Nadine Gordimer, José Saramago, Desmond Tutu and Canada's own John Polanyi – warned that, as a society, we need to reconsider the meaning of security. "What is lacking," wrote Polanyi in a later statement published in *The Globe and Mail*, "is a sense of urgency.... Unless we recognize that the future...depends on the good of all [the well-being of the poor countries of the world and the well-being of the rich countries of the world], the coming years will bring escalating conflict."[9] We need to take stock and learn the lessons that events have thrust upon us. This is true of nations and businesses and communities and churches and families and individuals.

Young people may decide to refocus on how they want to contribute to the world in the light of current events. Parents may want to reconsider the preparedness of their children for the world that is emerging. Business leaders may want to consider what could be different in the world of commerce. Life partners may want to consider how to make their relationships more life-giving. Families may want to re-evaluate whether their current activities make a difference to the soul as distinct from the body. Churches may want to take more seriously their mission to the spiritually hungry in their communities.

New Zealander Sir Peter Blake was the world's most celebrated sailor. He secured the America's Cup for his country twice. He was the only man to have completed five Whitbread around-the-world races, actually winning the race in 1990. In 1994, he circled the globe in a record 74 days, 22 hours, 17 minutes, and 22 seconds. This was one amazing person. His worst fear? That he would fall overboard in the night somewhere at sea. And what should befall him as his boat was anchored in a port in Brazil, but an encounter with pirates who shot him dead. On the day of his death, Peter Blake wrote in his log, "Our aim is to begin to understand the reasons why we must all start appreciating what we have before it is too late." John the baptizer couldn't have said it any better.

John's times were not so different than our own. He was surrounded by change just as we are. Let us take inventory, then. Let us take stock. Let the wolf in us live with the lamb; let the leopard in us lie down with the kid; let the calf and the young lion in us feed together. Let us find the new thing we are being drawn toward, even at the failing of the light. And then, let's get ready for something better.

One year, in desperation, I wondered out loud what would happen if a person like John were to appear in the community I was serving. I tried to speculate what kind of quality this man would have to have for everybody in the community to go down to the local river and receive his baptism. I ignored the fact that in that particular community, Taber, in southern Alberta, the Old Man River was just about frozen at that time of year and would induce hypothermia in anyone brave enough to dip into it. Wouldn't you know, a 90-year-

old man came up to me after I preached the sermon to
tell me that in the 1930s someone actually *had* lived by
the river, wore a long white beard and strange clothes,
and people *had* wondered whether he was some kind of
holy man, fool, or prophet.

In our day, we tend to admire people who are passionate. They give so much life to our lives. People of
faith are also often passionate. I don't think I'd be over-
stating things if I were to say that people of faith and
people of passion sometimes think they know exactly
what the world needs and set about convincing people
that they are right! They really believe that passion can
change people.

What people of passion sometimes lack, however, is
the ability to reflect on their own actions, which is precisely the corrective John the baptizer provides. In order to let spirit in, whatever that may mean to us, we
need to first let go. When people of faith combine passion with reflection, something interesting often takes
place. Upon reflection, we may realize that when we
charge out of the barricades to change others we rarely
succeed. More often, the reflective person discovers that
the changes that occur happen within their own heart.
We change our minds about ourselves. And that's the
most important thing.

The late Elie Wiesel, a true prophet of our times,
told the story of a just man who decided he must save
the world starting with Sodom, the most sinful of all
cities.

He was young, energetic, he had imagination, he had courage, (he had passion), he thought he knew how to go about it.

He came to Sodom and he went around the city from marketplace to marketplace, from school to school, from gathering place to gathering place with his picket saying to men and women and children: "Do not steal, do not kill, do not be hypocrites, do not be selfish, do not, do not, do not."

[In] the beginning people looked at him and listened even. They were amused because how many just [persons] happen to come to Sodom? It was not such a nice place. It wasn't such an appealing place. It was even a dangerous place for a just [person]. So they looked at him, but after a while they stopped looking and they stopped listening. Still, he went on shouting, reminding people to be human.

Many many years later he was stopped by a child in the street and the child said, "Poor stranger, poor teacher: Why are you doing all this? Don't you see it's useless?"

"Yes," said the old man.

"Then why do you continue?"

"I'll tell you," said the old man. "In the beginning I was convinced that if I were to shout loud enough, I would manage to change them. Now I know I will never change them. But if I continue shouting louder and louder with all my passion and all my strength it is because I don't want them to change me."[10]

The season of Advent before the winter solstice is a time for the passionate and reflective soul to let go the need to charge out of the barricades to change others.

Advent calls us to prepare a highway for change in our own hearts. People in our culture become very generous at this time of year. It's quite wonderful. People are open to new hopes and dreams. Faith is given a little more weight than doubt, hope is given more credence than frustration, peace is given more standing than conflict, and healing seems somehow a little more possible. During these few weeks, the world seems like it really could be a better place.

After worship one morning during Advent, I heard sirens across the street from the church I was serving. The sirens stopped at the apartment I could see from the front steps. The church treasurer and I were the only ones left in the building; everyone else had gone home. The treasurer suggested I drop by the apartment to see if assistance was needed. I said to myself, "Haven't I done my bit for today? I've preached a sermon. Shaken hands. Prayed for the faithful." Now, if I learned anything in my years as a minister it was always to listen to my church treasurer. Nevertheless, on that occasion – it was before the beginning of wisdom – I found myself in my car, headed toward home. And then a fire truck passed me and then the police car. Before I knew what was happening, I found myself behind a police car at the entrance to the apartment. There had been a death, a suicide. I was needed.

Thus began one of the most grace-filled experiences of my ministry. I led a deeply divided and embittered family into the presence of their dead brother and son to say their goodbyes, to vent their anger, and to find something they had not expected – reconciliation. It was a powerful moment and I discovered something I needed to learn about myself. I repented. I changed my mind. I went to help. I was helped. I saw differences in myself. I was changed.

Only when we have straightened our own pathways, only when we have given up the impossible task of straightening others' pathways, can we make space to change our own hearts.

Life is full of these riches. We can change our minds, let in the light, make a straighter path, level the valleys and hills a bit. We can refine our own parade toward the better.

WHO ARE THE PROPHETS OF OUR TIMES?

Prepare yourselves. Take a bath. Straighten up your house. Replace the broken things with whole things. Reconcile. Forgive. Forget the crooked highways of the past and get on the straighter road. Even in your wilderness, even in your calamity look up and clear the way.

In this procession called Advent, it may be our business to familiarize ourselves with the cadences of the prophetic voice. But who are the prophets in our day, and how do we recognize them? For some people, John the baptizer may be the prophet voice they are able to hear. But how can those who are less familiar or less comfortable with John's language, less familiar or less comfortable with the language of the church, discern the prophetic voices in their midst, the call to be better human beings? We need to be able to recognize and then internalize the prophetic message around us here and now.

And to be clear, there *are* prophetic voices in our lives. It's a given. You might find your prophet across the coffee table or the dinner table, on the bus, or in a lineup. A prophetic message for you may be delivered by a friend you have known for years, or by a stranger who catches you unawares; it could be in an email, or a text. It may come through someone you have initially dismissed. But no matter how it comes, it needs to be a truly personal encounter.

There are at least two things to be aware of here. The first is your instinct to dismiss the person and the message as foolish. At the same time, you will be struck by a kind of eloquence. You will notice the words, the way they are put together, the way they are delivered, the way heart speaks to heart. You will be captivated; you will be warmed, charmed in a particular way. Your prophet will be eloquent with their words or eloquent in their silence at just the right time.

A part of you might be dismissive and call them foolish, but another part will pay attention. Their words will help you envision alternatives, more helpful scenarios than you are able to imagine yourself, or have imagined up to this point.

This is one of the great values of community compared to the isolation so many of us experience. The prophetic voice guides us to be our better self, to get on that straighter highway, to get in the parade with the best of those who came before us.

The other thing to be aware of is that we may not want to hear what the prophet tells us. Remember Shakespeare's final line in *King Lear*: "The weight of this…time we must obey; speak what we feel, not what we ought to say."

The message hurts a little. It's *too* true, in a way.

Here's an example of a contemporary prophet's message. It may surprise you. It's a letter from a daughter to her mother. They have had the usual North American fight about the state of the daughter's bedroom. This is what the daughter wrote.

Dear Mom:

I have decided that you are the casualty in the "Battle of the Bedroom," not me. Yes, my bedroom is a mess. Yes, it is true you do not ask me to do much. But will wars end because I make my bed? Will all hunger in the world disappear because I hang up my clothes? With all the wonderful and terrible things happening in the world today, what does the condition of my bedroom matter?

Yes, I know that before the world can be put in order, people must put their own little world in order. But dust doesn't bother my world. To put my world in order, I need love, not Ajax cleanser. So, Mom, I'll make you a deal. You use a little more love and a I'll use a little more Ajax.[11]

What is it about this letter that makes the parent in me want to sit up and take notice? It is full of the prophetic, full of eloquence, full of heart. And it hurts all of us just a little, doesn't it? It even violates the unwritten rule that children ought never to instruct their parents on the better habits of love. A little like the best characters in Shakespeare's *King Lear*.

In recent times there has been an even more poignant teaching of parents by their children. After the massacre of 17 of their schoolmates at Marjory Stoneman Douglas High School in Parkland, Florida, students used their considerable talents on social media to organize a nation-wide walkout of classrooms. Under pressure from this same group, the governor of Florida signed a bill into law raising the minimum age to purchase a firearm to 21, and extended the waiting period to three days.

Who is your prophet? Who foretells the coming of newness? Your friend? Your partner? Your child? Your ex? Your grandchild? The stranger on the bus? The woman behind you at the hockey game? The man beside you on the park bench?

Advent is about getting ready for the new to come. Our role is to listen more and speak less, to let the message of our prophets make room in our hearts for a better self and better world.

NOTES

1.   Frye, *Collected Works*, 243.

2.   Frye, *Double Vision*, 3–16.

3.   Ibid., 17.

4.   Ibid., 17–18.

5. Northrop Frye, *Northrop Frye on Shakespeare*, ed. Robert Sandler (Markham: Fitzhenry & Whiteside, 1986, 1989), 111.
6. Herbert O'Driscoll, "From the Slave Pens of the Delta," in *Voices United* (Etobicoke, ON: The United Church Publishing House, 1996), #690.
7. Frye, *Shakespeare*, 116.
8. Frye, *Collected Works*, 244–252, specifically the Merry Christmas messages from Canadian Forum 1946–1949.
9. John Polyani, "Stupidity is the enemy: idealism is our only hope," in *The Globe and Mail*, December 7, 2001.
10. "Words from a Witness," *Conservative Judaism*, vol. 21 no. 3 (Spring 1967), 48. This text is taken from a PBS documentary on Wiesel. The outline of the story is also printed in *The Christian Science Monitor,* June 18, 1981.
11. Earnest Larson, *You Try Love and I'll Try Ajax* (Liguori, Mo: Liguori Press, 1969).

CHRISTMAS

The story of Christmas...is in part a story
of how [we], by cowering together in a common
fear of menace, discovered a new fellowship,
in fellowship a new hope, and in hope
a new vision of society.
— Northrop Frye, *Collected Works*[1]

FOR THE ENTIRE PERIOD OF MY TIME in pastoral ministry from 1981 to 2008, I thought that Christmas, the shortest season of the church year, was the one time when Christianity came closest to a true dialogue with the larger culture around it, or at least the time of year when the church had the half-cocked ear of the culture. According to Northrop Frye, this only *appears* to be the case: "Our very complaints about the hypocritical commercializing of the Christmas spirit prove that, for they show how vigorously Christmas can flourish without the smallest admixture of anything that could reasonably be called Christian."[2]

ANXIETY ABOUT THE SUN

Christmas is far older than Christianity or even the pre-Christian Yule and the Saturnalia of the Romans. Christmas is really an extension of an ancient and deep-seated emotional response to the winter solstice, our anxiety about the primal threat that the sun is going to give up on us, or be gobbled up by some unknown menacing monster.

If we think the relative strength of the sun is a minor matter for the human race, consider the mammoth effort ancient Britons put into Stonehenge. That was some cost-benefit analysis! And who can deny that when we heard for the first time that our sun actually has a limited life span and will eventually burn itself out four billion or so years from now, it awakened in the deepest part of ourselves a primal dread we have always felt as a species. The sun loves us. The sun does not love us. Let's make a bargain with the sun. We continue to walk on the eggshells of this persistent anxiety.

Nowadays it is not only shown by our display of lights and stuffing ourselves at Christmas, it is also shown by what the therapeutic community calls SAD, or Seasonal Affective Disorder. It is all, at bottom, a busy avoidance of our worst fears in our own time. But our attempts at avoidance don't really work. As the marketing guru Seth Godin says somewhere, "Anxiety is experiencing failure in advance." In this case, the "advance" or future we fear is beyond the likely survival of the human race itself. No matter: anxiety around the loss of the sun resides genetically in the collective gut of the human.

If Advent, the time of year before the solstice, is about reflection and self-correction as we contemplate how we function in the two orders of nature – Frye's discussion of what we are like at our best and worst – and if it's also a remembrance of the parade of which we and those who came before us are a part, the time immediately after Advent, Christmas, is about community-building and the hope that comes from it. Or at least it *could* be. Christmas *could* be about so much more than the office party, or attending Christmas Eve services, or even the family gathering around the brightly lit tree and the dinner table groaning with food and the bright red colours of the season. Surely it could be more than a moment in time when we mark a few days after the solstice only to forget about it all until the carols start playing in the mall after the next Halloween.

There is no doubt that the Christmas season in the context of the church has provided the culture with many wonders, including timeless music (the carols, the masses, Handel's *Messiah*), universal narratives (shepherds, angels, the Magi), and truly well-intentioned sentiment (peace on earth, goodwill to all people). Year after year in 27 years of service to the church, I felt inspired and newly motivated by the impetus the Christian celebration of Christmas provided. It was exhausting, but at the same time exhilarating. In a sense, it kept me going. It pulled me through the ensuing year.

Since my partner and I left the safety of the institutional church, community is the thing we miss the most. Not that we couldn't have stayed in it, as we tried to do after we left our pastorates. What we found over time, however, is that the Christian frame on time, spirituality, and community felt overly restrictive. In the years since we've left the ministry and the institutional church, we have struggled to think through and seek out alternatives, so far with little to show for our efforts.

No one needs to convince us of the benefits of community nor of the hope it provides. We just need the communal spirit represented by or engendered at Christmas to be carried forward throughout the year, as well as a conscious and concerted effort to encourage the culture to be more human and more compassionate, as befits the fools from the higher level of nature that we try to be. From our point of view, the church spends far too much of its time, energy, and resources on self-preservation.

But perhaps this is the wrong way to think about community. It may be that the Christmas impetus is less about finding the community and hope we *don't* have, and more about appreciating the community we *already* have, and finding hope in that. The community could be family – biological or chosen – for example. After all, the universal message hidden in the Christian concept of incarnation is that God, however one conceives of God, has been born into human community, and, if we care to believe the first chapter of John's gospel, this has been true from the beginning: "In the beginning the Word already was. The Word was in God's presence..." (John 1:1–3).

If we think of Word here as communication at its most profound, the deep connection that comes from a joining by linguistic means or human tenderness, the Word cannot be restricted, even in a biblical sense, to a moment in time when a person was born. And if the Word was in God's presence at the beginning of creation, surely the Word was a presence in God too.

All of this is a way of saying that community itself – being present to one another in profound communicative ways – has a holiness built into it, a power for good, a light shining in whatever darkness humans can and do create for one another. This spirit was echoed in a *New York Times* article by the Dalai Lama and Arthur C. Brooks. "Start each day," they advised, "By consciously asking ourselves, 'What can I do today to appreciate the gift that others offer me?'"[3] The assumption behind this worthwhile, counterintuitive activity is that we already have community to appreciate; we just don't engage in it. This is the essence of the Christmas message behind all Christmas messages.

CINDY AT THE MALL

I remember the day that the incarnation was born in me. I was sitting in a shopping mall the week before Christmas. Across from me sat a young woman named Cindy – at least I'll call her Cindy. We were sitting at one of those plastic tables just big enough for a cup of coffee and a doughnut. The chairs we sat in were meant to be uncomfortable and they were, encouraging us not to stay too long – like a church pew.

Cindy wasn't a day over 15. Yet she looked much older. She was pregnant. She had no place to call home. An acquaintance had called me out of the blue and had asked if I would meet her at the mall, amidst the passing smell of wet wool, people in their muddy boots and winter coats clutching Christmas packages, their irritability swirling in the air behind them in eddies. Cindy told me about the man who didn't care, and about her mother, who had found her own man and who didn't want her around. She told me of her shame.

I couldn't help thinking of another 15-year-old mother-to-be, troubled as Cindy was troubled, puzzled, and poor. Mary would have been 15 years old if she was a day. She may have been younger. I like the unglorified, undeified version of the story because it doesn't whitewash the shame. The unglorified version is, to me, the most powerful. It speaks to me of courage. It says to me that all of us are capable of courage in such times. It says to me that nothing will be impossible if we have the will in community.

Cindy was alive to a promise being made in her. For she spoke, like Mary, of the promise, of a gift: "Here I am, Lord, your servant; let it be according to your word." It may have been the naïve courage of a 15-year-old, but God had rewarded naïve courage before. What is absent in the Mary story is the role community, aside from Joseph – who against all the expectations and demands of the society of his day chose to stay with Mary – played in what Mary chose to do. Though no mention is made of the role of community in Mary's decision, it was clear to me that it was incumbent upon the community I represented to support Cindy in her discernment, and through whatever choice she would make.

Cindy was not clear what she should do. Like Mary, like Israel, like Jesus, like all of us when we are faced with a cross in our lives, Cindy needed to "dwell in the wilderness awhile and find her freedom there," to paraphrase Herbert O'Driscoll's hymn "From the Slave Pens of the Delta."[4]

The world may empty us, but she knew community could fill her up again, and so it would. Cindy made Mary come alive for me, and she made Christmas a more awakening experience for me. So whether for me alone, or for her and me together, or for the community that was called to nurture her in their goodness, the word was made flesh and dwelt amongst us. I walked into the gathering blizzard outside.

MARY, THE BIBLE, AND TRUTH

Those who think the Bible is a history book want to know if things "actually happened," to which the sensitive observer replies, as did Northrop Frye, "nothing in the Bible which may be historically accurate is there because it is historically accurate. It's a book about faith and discernment and transformation."[5]

Here's another way to look at it. We all know that

Thomas Edison invented the phonograph. What you may not know is that he was also the head of the first record company and, to the great chagrin of his officials, to the end of his days he insisted on choosing each song and every singer for every release. I say *chagrin* because although in his later years Edison was completely deaf he was quite convinced that he could detect the most beautiful voice by looking at the grooves in a record through a magnifying glass! Edison would hold the vinyl up to the glass and scrutinize the pattern of scratches in each groove. This is often how we view the Bible. We look at the grooves and we don't hear the music![6]

I have some sympathy for those who need the history to be accurate. But you cannot demand from a story more than it will bear, and the Christmas story invites us to be *transformed*. It does *not* invite us to be *convinced*. It invites us to hear the music.

Before the Enlightenment, when we really got into arguments, lists, categories, proofs, and so on, people actually valued those who saw visions. In the time of Dante, for example, visions were considered a significant, interesting, and disciplined kind of dreaming. We have almost lost that sense. The story of Mary invites us back, which may be why she is more venerated now than she was even in Dante's time – because this is a story that calls us to the deepest part of ourselves and we want to get back to that place. Not the place where superstition and religion tyrannize us, but where visions help us live! Mary's story suggests history, but even more it suggests mystery. It invites transformation, not conviction. It's not about the grooves; it's about the music.

Well, what about Mary? She has inspired the best in human culture to spring up in her honour. Chartres along with countless other churches and cathedrals were inspired by her. Her name is attached to the best in poetry. Dante placed her in the highest heaven and wrote a poem of sublime beauty to her to complete his master work, *The Divine Comedy*. Some of the most famous paintings are an attempt to capture what God challenged her to do. She is venerated in beautiful music. She has been called the new Eve, the Queen of Heaven.

It's hard to explain why all this for a simple peasant woman. Was she crafty like Cleopatra, who tore an empire in two? Not really. Was she beautiful like Helen of Troy, who launched a thousand ships? We don't know. Was she a leader like Queen Elizabeth the First, who defended and enriched a has-been nation? There is no evidence that she was a leader. Was she a mystic like Teresa of Avila? We don't even know *that*, although many would assume that she was. Aramaic, her native language, had no feminine form for words like pious and upright.[7]

"When the time had come," wrote Teilhard de Chardin, "when God resolved to realize God's incarnation before our eyes, God had first of all to raise up in the world a virtue capable of drawing God as far as ourselves ... What did God do? [God]... called forth on earth an integrity so great that, within this transparency, God would concentrate Godself to the point of appearing as a child."[8]

Perhaps it *is* all about integrity. Mary did the simplest thing, and yet the most profound thing. She did what all faithful people hope to do; she saw what God intended for her and let it be accomplished, and then she had the courage to suffer and rejoice in the consequences.

Between the lines of the wonderful account in Luke's gospel there is revealed a tremendous courage. It is this intertwining of mystery and courage and integrity that I think can help us. Consider the details of the story, for despite what I just said about history and mystery, even the "facts" push us toward mystery. Maybe that's why the story still captivates us. So here are the grooves, as it were.

It is hard to imagine a person who had so little promise for influence in her time, much less in *all* time, as Mary. She was a simple peasant girl of 14 or 15 living as a Jew in a Palestine dominated by a hated and brutal conqueror. Mary was probably one of many young women of her village, a bit frail looking, barefoot, in clothes soiled and torn.[9]

She was promised or betrothed to an older man named Joseph. It was an arranged marriage. When a couple in that time were betrothed, it meant that they had been formally promised to one another at a ceremony, where, in all likelihood, they would have met and seen one another for the first time. And then there would have been a six-month waiting period before they actually started living together. In the intervening time, they would not have seen each other at all. In fact, Mary would have been sequestered behind closed doors with her family.

It is in that time between the ceremony of betrothal and their formal coming together that the scene, described in scripture and by so many in song and in paint, took place. The power of that story has built cathedrals, empowered the poor, sustained the sick, and given strength to the dying. What *really* happened, we do not know. Perhaps Mary offered a meal to a beggar and the beggar was an angel. That's how José Saramago imagines it in his book *The Gospel According to Jesus Christ*.[10] Perhaps something more sinister took place.

Naturally and tragically, people of the village would have thought the worst. Historically, we know something unusual happened, for the gospel is at pains to make sense of what makes no sense, which is a good indication that something unusual is true. The fact that there was controversy may be the only real history we know about Jesus' family.

This pregnancy was only the beginning of Mary's torment and, curiously, the beginning of her joy at the same time. Remember that at that time the community's opinion of you meant everything. You were nobody if the community thought you were nobody; you were somebody if the community thought you were somebody. You were tried by gossip in the court of opinion in the village, whether it was informed or not. If you were pregnant before the arranged marriage was consummated, you were an adulteress. There could be no other earthly explanation. The penalty for adultery was death and everlasting shame for your family. To retain your self-assurance and self-confidence in the face of the condemnation of your small community under these circumstances would be truly extraordinary. This is grace under pressure. This is courage.[11] This is integrity.

In one sense, Mary's fate was in Joseph's hands. He was the "wronged" party. Would he leave her to the vagaries of public opinion? It would seem that his first instinct was to do just that, to leave her to her family and the judgment of the community. But in this case her very life would have been in danger. He thought of a better alternative.

Many would have called him a fool. He might have been the brunt of off-colour jokes and ridicule. But, somehow, he too discerned that the most difficult thing was what he was meant to do. Joseph was being called to another alternative. Mary was being called to another alternative. They discerned, like many people of integrity, that *this* is what they were born to do.

Perhaps they went back to Joseph's home town, Bethlehem, to escape the shame. Perhaps word of their predicament preceded them and no one would give them shelter. It is not too hard for us to see why a stable would have been the only place for such a birth, and why an escape to Egypt would have followed – a new start in a new community that did not know the mysterious and scandalous story.

This part of the Christmas story, Mary and Joseph's story, tells of ordinary people trying to work out what is intended for them. The working out of that intention is cloaked in tragedy, joy, and mystery all wrapped in one. They did not know the details of the future. They just knew that they had been set on a right path, which would not be an easy one. There would be many joys and many sorrows. They would need courage and resilience. This is their story and it is our story, too. Essentially, it is a story about the possibility that resides in an integrated, communicative, trusting community, even a community of two. But even in saying two we know intuitively that they were not alone.

There is an intention for us, too, in the Christmas season, in that period just after the winter solstice. The intention for us here is also cloaked in the inexplicable: in mystery, tragedy, and joy. We don't know the details either. We don't know what the results of that intention will be. We can't know the future. But we can hope in community. We can be transformed by the promise that pre-exists in us and, in that integrity, we can hear the music and see the beauty of life even as we struggle, even as confusion reigns around us. We can refuse to be bent by darkness. We can create instead of destroy. We can hold out the hand of friendship when others hold out the hand of hate. We can promote healing when there is division. We can hope when others despair. This is the "intention" I speak about. And these too are extraordinary things. These too are miracles.

Community can do anything with any life: Mary's life, Joseph's life, Jesus' life, even with my life and yours. And nothing will be impossible.

ONE WONDERFUL NIGHT

One night. One baby. One child. One young life. Every year in every community, faithful, wondering people gather in churches to celebrate the birth of one baby, a baby who, over time, came to represent or exemplify our hope.

Christmas is one of those celebrations that had to arise as the Christian gospel became more established in hearts and minds. Throughout the centuries, as our culture got used to Jesus' idea that God is not some distant landlord who never visits but instead is the friend who leads us forward, there had to be a day in which the arrival of this precious truth could be celebrated. And it wasn't just some propaganda tool put forward by church-types. Far from it.

As the Christian church began to celebrate Christmas on one wonderful night, it realized that the faith Jesus preached was in some sense the faith of people's experience. Christmas after Christmas, Christians found that when they put their trust in community and not only in themselves, they were rewarded with something that was nothing like a new car or a doll under the Christmas tree, but something that they did not expect, something that made them better.

There was a moment in my life when I decided that I would never have children, even though something very deep inside me had taught me that was all I should ever want. But there were many people in my life and many people whom I admired in history who were childless – Northrop Frye being only one – and I set about channelling my energy into alternatives. For me, it was a trust issue. I trusted that there was another purpose for me, and I set to find out what that was.

Now it is not always the case that we are given later what we think we've given up. The outcome might have been very different. But fate is full of irony, and so now, these many years later, I have two children of my own. Are they more beloved to me now having "given them up" so to speak, so long ago? Absolutely. And who knows, when children are given, how long they are yours and you theirs. The thing is, one learns from these experiences to trust not in our best-laid plans, not in the expected outcome, but that as you let yourself be held by your community, such as it is, the miraculous *does* happen. And, over time, this kind of trust becomes a lifestyle. Experience speaks to experience, which speaks to experience, and gradually we learn about a life that can be marked by some kind of confidence.

People gather in churches on Christmas Eve because somewhere, perhaps even in the far reaches of their life's experience, they too trusted and were rewarded with substantive hope. A life. A person. Healing. Wisdom.

It is not surprising that with this experience over time, people would mark their lives on one night. On Christmas Eve, people remember the previous Christmas, and the year before that. People remember back to the time someone died; or to a truth someone told; or to the Christmas when they were 12, when they stood at the top of the stairs and saw the tree and the lights and the people, and they heard the laughter and smelled the spruce and the cedar, and warm tears fell on their soft slippers and they realized that sadness comes with joy, and joy with sadness. That's when the warm mystery became real – the death, the loss, the finding, the change. Christmas helps us mark the passage of time.

Nestled in the tumultuousness of the season and the night and the loss and the change is this warm glow at the centre, this light, this shining, this hope. Not blind hope, no. But hope the substance of which we have experienced in our lives when, having given up control, we found new ground upon which to stand, substantial hope that points toward the future.

One night. One baby born in Bethlehem, one young life, one child – the representative substance of community and hope.

THE VISIT OF THE WISE

Apparently, in a parallel universe, there were actually wise women who greeted the Messiah. In contrast to the wise men, however, they called ahead, asked someone for directions, arrived on time, brought a casserole and appropriate gifts, delivered the baby, cleaned the stable, and, in that universe, there is still peace and goodwill on earth.

Be that as it may, something extraordinary happened even in *this* universe, such as it is. There were remarkable astronomical phenomena in the period around the birth of Jesus: Haley's comet for one, and the conjunction of Jupiter and Saturn. And there are historical records in the first century of potentates from the East bringing regal gifts to Jerusalem and Rome.[12] It was hot news on everyone's lips, like when a pope or a monarch visits today. Who's to say, then, that there may not have been a side trip to Bethlehem? Who's to say that they didn't know something the rest of Palestine just let go by.

Before I go any further, I should say that in the calendar of the church year, the visit of the wise men to the infant Jesus is the story that begins the Epiphany season. Although I will refer to it again in the next chapter, I want to include it here as well because the story so often gets told at Christmas, when it is conflated with the story of the shepherds.

In any event, it's fascinating that, as the story goes, the wise ones weren't Jews, they weren't Greeks, they weren't Romans ... they were Persians. They were from the area which is present-day Iraq and Iran. They might have been wise men, as our tradition assumes; they might have been astronomers or philosophers; they might have been magicians or astrologers. The "three kings" tradition actually dates from St. Francis; he's the one who put that spin on the story.

When the first Christian church was built in Bethlehem, the Emperor Constantine decorated it with a fresco depicting Persian wise men. The wise men are dressed in Persian clothes. In 614 C.E., the armies of Chosroes of the Sassanid dynasty of Persian kings swept over Palestine, wreaking havoc and setting churches to the torch. But they spared the Bethlehem church because the soldiers recognized their own countrymen.[13]

I think it is helpful to have the story of the wise men in Matthew read after Christmas – at its proper point as the story that launches the Epiphany season – because it provides such a contrast to the Lukan story. As Frye points out in an article that appeared in "Canadian Forum" in December 1949, the Lukan story is full of sweetness and light: angels and shepherds and the manger; peace and goodwill to all people. In contrast, the story in Matthew is quite gloomy. Here is a tale of

a jealous tyrant who filled the land with dead children and wailing mothers, while [the] wise men escaped from the country in one direction and the Holy Family in another. It is a tale in which all the characters except the tyrant and his minions are either murdered or refugees. Today we know as never before that this, too, is part of the Christmas story. But the story of Luke, with the shepherds and the manger and the angels... does not cease to be true because the story in Matthew is also true. The story of Christmas...is, in part a story of how ... [people] discovered a new fellowship...a new hope ... [during dark times].[14]

In his wonderful poem "The Journey of the Magi," T. S. Eliot has one of the Magi reflecting on his journey from the distance of time. So, like the memories of any journey, it becomes more remarkable in retrospect. V. S. Naipaul said somewhere, "A journey to a foreign land is completely unspectacular until it is behind you." From this vantage point, Eliot seems to collapse the birth of Jesus, the reign of death caused by Herod, and the death of Jesus into a single earth-changing calamity that brought permanent change and hope to the human community. Eliot talks about the simultaneity of birth and death, that death is a kind of birth and birth a kind of death too.[15]

A shining star on a dark canopy shows us how to understand the presence of hope in a troubled world. The story tells us that hope is not obvious. Hope is not in your face like a winter snowstorm. We have to look for it. We have to look up from the street of our everyday concerns. But once we have looked and once we have found this star, it is always a presence for us in whatever darkness we might encounter in our lives, as someone put it, "At the edges, where lines are blurred…"

On a dark week in November 2016, perhaps no city in North America felt the darkness more palpably than Montreal. The city learned that week that their most beloved and famous troubadour, Leonard Cohen, had died the day before Donald Trump was elected President of the United States. By the time the news of Cohen's death was released by the family that Thursday, he had already been buried in the Jewish rite of his ancestors. He was in his grave. As a shrine formed around his house in Montreal, the whole community was swept up in an overwhelming sadness.

My eldest child, a playwright in the city, described many scenes of tears and sorrow that week amongst those who were active in the arts. And yet there was a kind of power with which people were holding one another. This describes so well what an incarnational hope can be, not only in the Christian context but in the wider community as well.

Hope is not found in the sameness of our easy chair. Hope calls us up, out of the comfortable country in which we reside and moves us to places we do not know, and possibly to places we do not even want to know, even to places we fear to know. The wise ones left their homes and went into a foreign land to seek the answer to their hearts' deepest desire. They went out from themselves to unknown territory. They risked and they hoped at the same time.

Isn't it interesting that we tend to believe that our answers lie in the safety of sameness? But in many of the great stories of the world, including Homer's *Odyssey*, truth and learning are more apt to be found on a journey away from home, where a lot is up for grabs and there is much uncertainty.

As the holidays come to an end, something – I don't know, maybe it's all that turkey – invites a kind of inertia in us. It's hard to get off the chair. We call it cocooning. The holiday is wonderful. Being with family. Padding about in slippers. Getting dressed when we feel like it. The "answer" we've been seeking seems to be at home. But this story gets us out of the house. Hope is not obvious; we need to look. Hope calls us out of comfort to a journey that we may not appreciate until it is over. The wise ones were seeking. They were seeking the same thing we seek: answers to the puzzling dilemma of being alive in the times in which we've been placed, in the place we've been given. They did it by following a star on the black canopy of the night sky, in a dark time, confident that something, they did not know what, would lead them somewhere they needed to be.

NOTES

1. Frye, *Collected Works*, 252.
2. Ibid., 244.
3. "Dalai Lama: Behind our Anxiety," *New York Times*, November 4, 2016.
4. O'Driscoll, "Slave Pens."
5. Frye, *Collected Works*, 6.
6. My thanks to my friend Paul Taylor for this story.
7. José Saramago, *The Gospel According to Jesus Christ* (New York: Harcourt Brace and Co., 1994), 15–16.
8. Teilhard de Chardin, *The Divine Milieu*, trans. Sîon Cowell (Brighton: Sussex University Press, 2004), 96–97.
9. This is Saramago's description. I find it the most moving, the most prophetic and the most true. Saramago, *Gospel*, 15–16.
10. Ibid., 17–18.

11. Ernest Hemingway defined courage as grace under pressure. See John F. Kennedy, *Profiles in Courage* (New York: Pickle Partners, 2015), 13.

12. Raymond E. Brown, *The Birth of the Messiah: A Commentary on the Infancy Narratives in Matthew and Luke* (New York: Image Books, 1979), 189.

13. Ibid., 168.

14. Frye, *Collected Works*, 252.

15. T. S. Eliot, "The Journey of the Magi," in *The Complete Poems and Plays 1909–1950* (New York: Harcourt, Brace & Company, 1971), 68.

EPIPHANY

The really significant events of human life
are hidden from view when they occur.
– Northrop Frye, *Collected Works*[1]

IN THE CHRISTIAN YEAR, the season of Epiphany fills the gap between Christmas and Lent. In churches, it is the lowest time of the year in terms of attendance, but in a sense it holds more riches than any other season, especially from Northrop Frye's point of view.

In the Western tradition, Epiphany day (January 6) is synonymous with the story of the Magi's visit to the infant Jesus after following a miraculous star – a story we've already referred to in the previous chapter. As Matthew tells the story, the star is a light that shines against a very dark canopy of murder, betrayal, and exile. Still, the word epiphany means "reveal" and what the season reveals, including the star narrative, are the various ways the New Testament shows that Jesus is God's intervention in nature in general (the star and later the descent of a dove), and in the affairs of humans in particular (as when, at a wedding banquet, Jesus turns water into wine).

But as Frye explains the phenomenon, we need not get caught up in that doctrinal agenda unnecessarily. For Frye, the *revealing* or epiphany is found in the way language reveals unseen but insistent and persistent spiritual truths. This language is *insistent* in that it seeks our better understanding as it nudges us toward spiritual depth. The language is *persistent* in that, once read, it will not let us go. We want to go back to it again and again.[2]

According to Google, the word epiphany is used far more in our time than it ever has been in the past. Perhaps this is because, far from the spiritual wasteland it is reputed to be, our time is rich in a wider spiritual exploration even as churches decline and disappear. It may be that we are finally coming to realize that an understanding of a larger human freedom and the quest for a wider spiritual path are one and the same.

PERTURBING EVENTS

Who knows why he awoke at three o'clock in the morning? Why does anyone wake up at three o'clock in the morning? Maybe a car went by and it was the noise of spinning wheels on gravel that disturbed his sleep. Or maybe it was one of those dogs that never stops barking. Or maybe it was those ice cubes his partner calls feet; maybe they touched him in the middle of a dream and he thought he was freezing to death.

As it happened, during the time Frye was in bed an ice storm had blown in. Occasionally, ice storms occur in Ontario just at the beginning of autumn. At that time of year, they reap horrible damage on flora and fauna, even as an eerie beauty becomes the landscape. Anyway, it was three o'clock in the morning and Frye was decidedly wide awake. He got out of bed, for his mind was beginning to rev up as it usually did when he woke at such an ungodly hour and time began to pass like a caterpillar along a football field; he knew he wouldn't get back to sleep right away no matter how hard he tried.

For some reason known to no one, least of all himself, Frye decided to go to the window in front of the bed. He drew the curtains and there, in the luminous dark, he saw something that moved him like nothing else he had seen in a long while: two branches laden with icicles, one on each side of the window, each silhouetted against a field of snow. On one branch sat a cardinal, and on the other a blue jay.[3]

It was one of those special experiences when one dies a little bit in one moment to live more intensely going forward. Frye witnessed pure and unspeakable beauty, and it brought forth joy from within him! The experience arose from mere chance, no question, which was part of the mystery that pointed in the direction of the timeless or, more accurately, it's part of the mystery of how the timeless can intrude upon the present moment.

While Jesus walked this earth, the message he stated over and over again through his parables was that the kingdom of God is in the midst of us. It has taken centuries for us to understand what he meant by that. Scholars now believe that the kingdom of God that Jesus talked about was never meant as a *place*, even in the metaphorical sense, but as an *event* or as a series of events in our lives that prompt close attention. God, not as subject, Jesus seems to be saying, but God as a verb. God in that liminal space in-between the difficult times that invite transformation of the spirit, and alternative action. Often it is our response when the unexpected impinges upon us that is key.[4] The timeless intrudes upon our time, like a burglar in the night. The timeless clock puts our individual wristwatches out of time and into absurdity. We are receivers of a special favour not because we are special ourselves, but because the realm of the timeless has made us a gift. There has been an intrusion, welcome or not. There has been a revealing that offers us its attention, if we let it.

The trouble is that we are not generally content with the way the timeless breaks into our world, our own versions of Frye's nighttime epiphany notwithstanding. If the realm of the timeless broke in that way all the time, it would be easier to fathom, or so we think. But we prefer routine in our schedule; we want our wristwatch, our time. We want the timeless to be there in the way we think we need the most, at the time we choose. But all too often the timeless is not found there at all. In fact, we often face an icy silence during those times and we think God, which is often the name we use for timeless time, is dead.

Jesus' parables witness to the spiritual truth that when we ask, "Where is God?" we are expecting conformity to our time, and to our rules. The timeless wants to reveal itself to us *all* the time, but the trouble is we only want or expect it to happen in a place and at time when we're ready for it, or able to recognize it. It's a little like when you are getting ready to go somewhere and you give yourself plenty of time. To your surprise, you then find that you are ready a few minutes early. So you say, "Hey, I can relax for a few minutes." We call it a few moments of grace. But it's quite unlike the grace the parables illustrate.

It has been many years since President Anwar Sadat of Egypt was brutally assassinated. He was by no means a model leader. In some ways he was a ruthless tyrant. But he was also a peacemaker. Before Sadat, who would have thought that an Egyptian leader would ever set foot on Israeli soil and address the Israeli parliament? Who would have thought that these two bitter foes could come together around a peace table even for a fleeting moment? Sadat lived with the fear of assassination every single day. When asked by a reporter whether it worried him, he said, "I believe in God." He said, "I know that God will not let the bullet strike one second before my work here is finished." Of course, the bullet or bullets did strike, the action of God notwithstanding.

But what a way to live one's life! Every second he knew that his life was in danger, he also had trust.

That's grace! This is the true spirit of letting the time-less break in according to God's time and not our own. Of course, in Sadat's case, that attitude brought with it a troubling self-justification, but he almost got it. It is in the telling of his story from beginning to end that we surmise that he was right about God's action in the world.

According to Jesus' reckoning, grace comes when you've done your relaxing and you realize sometime later that you forgot to do an important thing. Let's say you forgot your wallet. The situation thrusts you into the unexpected, and a bit of anxiety. It is in this unex-pected moment that the timeless may intrude. This is when we need to let another part of ourselves pay atten-tion, even as we try to solve the immediate problem.

When I was in Grade 9, my teacher, Miss Muriel Sherring, was the person I respected most in the world. Miss Sherring used to say that she never married be-cause she was answering the door when the phone rang, or she was talking on the phone when there was a knock on the door. In other words, the moment didn't come at the right time. It was only much later that I realized that my revered teacher was saying to us that she hadn't had a handle on the right kind of time for romance and marriage. Perhaps she said this with regret, perhaps not. But she *did* imply that if she had had a handle on the timing, perhaps if she had let disorder encroach a bit, she might have been able to grasp what lay beyond her kind of time. What if she had attended to disorder a little more than she did?

What is actually required of us here? Being open to the timeless means being quiet; it means letting quiet in. But it also means letting the randomness in life speak to us about our lives. Maurice Boyd, a mentor of mine, told the story of when he was a child in Ireland. In his room he had a little tapestry on the wall with a saying embroidered onto it. The saying was about grace, but he didn't know what grace was; he was too young. What he *did* know is that his mother's name was Grace, and so he thought that the verse on the wall was about his mother.

It didn't matter. Because his mother taught him what grace was like. Grace, when it is most meaningful, comes like a mother's love, not just in the moments when we plan to receive that love, but in the special unplanned moments when love or care, or pause or the gift of time itself, is given to us when we did not expect it but needed it most. So often, we only realize the importance of those moments in retrospect. We can never plan such moments, because planning itself is an enemy of the experience.

After I left pastoral ministry, I had an opportunity to work in the Downtown Eastside of Vancouver. As I was completing my training to be a therapist, the folks who were running First United Church at the time invited me to work with the community. It was a very rich period of my life. Many epiphanies occurred, almost on a daily basis it seemed.

The winter of 2008 was a particularly brutal one and, at that time, homeless people were allowed into the sanctuary of First United during the day to sleep. They were very respectful of the sanctuary and of the furniture in it. People curled up on the pews around the chancel, and the pulpit and the communion table were not touched. I regularly did rounds of the pews to see if I could offer support through conversation. Sometimes people were awake and just sitting. I spoke with them.

One day on my first round, I noticed that the furniture had been moved to make room for more people in the choir loft and the chancel area. The communion table had been shifted to just inside the entrance, so it didn't appear to be altar-like as it usually did, and instead seemed just a piece of furniture. There, all curled up on its clean, clear expanse was a man, fast asleep. He hadn't known what it was. As I beheld the scene, what became clear to me was a deepening of what the sacrament of communion could actually mean.

Here, a body broken. Here, a body sheltered. Here, a body seeking and finding renewal. Here was Christ's body broken in the form of the body of the outcast. Suddenly, the sanitized version of communion practiced regularly in churches seemed shallow. Perhaps it was at that moment that I began to move away from organized religion. A disconnect had formed in my mind.

That disconnect was heightened a few years later when, out of a supposed concern for safety in that same sanctuary, a man named Gabriel was denied entry by the "principalities and powers." A refugee from Sudan, troubled by alcoholism and regularly picked up unconscious from the streets around the church, Gabriel had sought shelter in the church as he regularly did. But on that day and forever after, he was banned from the building. He was seen by many later that day sitting on the steps of First United with a loaf of dry bread in his hands, crying. He would be found dead in his bed not many months later.

Too often, we structure our lives in a way that discourages the unexpected. The Canadian philosopher George Grant said once that what we crave in North America is to shape the world as we want it. We want to master our lives as well, leaving no unknown variables, no rock in danger of being overturned. But there is a point at which the will to master our time comes into conflict with the breaking in of the timeless. No wonder God has died for so many people. We want God to work in our time and on our schedule. We want the timeless to take time for us, but we rarely take time for it. To do that, we need to account for the timeless in time, and we can only do that with hopeful hearts and a retrospective gaze.

It is when we live with hopeful hearts that we discover unexpected grace, when we experience joy. As William Blake's poem "Eternity" states,

He who binds to himself a joy
Does the winged life destroy
But he who kisses the joy as it flies
Lives in eternity's sunrise

Unexpected grace continually flies by us; it is forever flying by us. We need to kiss it as it flies and then, in the words we construct to remember it, we will wonder at its meaning.

When we consider the gifts we have already been given, isn't life itself the unexpected gift? When a woman finds that she is pregnant, there is a moment – and it doesn't seem to matter if the child was planned or not – when an unexpectedness about the news takes her breath away. Surprise breaks through everything that would prevent it. It intrudes and everything else falls away.

What is it like to enter the world as a newborn babe? Coming from a dark, warm place without any warning into the cold outside world. We cry at the surprise of being alive. The surprise of birth itself is a parable of the timeless presence in and around us. The moment of natural birth is always unexpected and yet the sheer wonder of it communicates to the parents and to everyone else a special, ephemeral quality to life.

The timeless sense comes unexpectedly in misfortune, too. This is the hardest grace to recognize, acknowledge, and accept – when we feel like the labourer who has been cheated out of what we are due, when equal work does not bring equal pay. Yet while we pause, grace may find us even in those times. The hopeful will even say, "especially in those times." The most inspiring people I've ever met are those who have found grace in difficult times.

In her memoir, *The Year of Magical Thinking*, American writer Joan Didion recounts the year that followed the sudden death of her husband, John Gregory Dunne. It is the most brutally honest treatment of grief I have ever read. Her candour is breathtaking. Didion strikes us as a nominal believer, at least on the surface. Although she makes reference to her Episcopalian roots and to Dunne's Roman Catholic roots, the memoir is not written from the perspective of church at all.

And yet the kind of grace we have been discussing is everywhere in evidence – not in her words so much as between the words, like the timeless itself. Didion's book itself is an act of hope, as it attempts to sort out the real from the illusory. This is what honesty does. This is how grace is found.

People who have recently lost someone have a certain look, recognizable maybe only to those who have felt such a shock themselves and have owned the shaking of the foundations that it truly is. The look is one of extreme vulnerability, nakedness, openness... The people who have lost someone look naked because they think themselves invisible. I myself felt invisible for a period of time, incorporeal.[5]

And then Didion draws forth the myth that captures the experience.

I seem to have crossed one of those legendary rivers that divide the living from the dead, entered a place in which I could be seen only by those who were themselves recently bereaved. I understood for the first time the power in the

image of the rivers, the Styx, the Lethe, the cloaked ferry-
man with his pole. I understood for the first time the meaning in the practice of suttee. Widows did not throw themselves on the burning raft out of grief. The burning raft was
instead an accurate representation of the place to which
their grief (not their families, not the community, not
custom, their grief) had taken them. On the night John
died we were thirty-one days short of our fortieth anniversary... I wanted more than a night of memories and sighs.

I wanted to scream.

I wanted him back.[6]

Karl Marx taught us how faith could be an "opiate to
the masses," lulling people into a disastrous acquies-
cence. Friedrich Nietzche taught that faith can con-
strain us to a childlike and unhelpful dependency.
Sigmund Freud showed us that the "oceanic feeling"
could be different aspects of our interiority at war. Joan
Didion has helped us separate our anger, and the "magical
thinking" to which it attaches, from our pain. All are
prophets to the honest spiritual pilgrim.

The southern American writer Flannery O'Connor
wrote a letter to a friend. O'Connor was a woman who
knew the torment of physical pain. For a good part of
her life she had Lupus. It attacked her legs and she
could not walk without crutches. But she wrote to her
friend, "I have never been anywhere but sick. In a sense
sickness is a place, more instructive than a long trip to
Europe, and it's always a place where there's no company, where nobody can follow. Sickness before death

is a very appropriate thing and I think those who don't have it miss one of God's mercies."[7]

This is truly unusual. How is it possible to expect God's grace in suffering? And yet it is in suffering that the spontaneous nature of life and death become real to us. Jesus repeatedly tells us that it is in those times that the timeless is closest.

Thomas Merton learned to find God in silence and contemplation. When he finally became comfortable with the contemplative life, he received ordination. This, he thought, was the outward recognition that he had achieved some intimacy with God. But then he got sick. "When the summer of my ordination ended," he wrote, "I found myself face to face with a mystery that was beginning to manifest itself in the depths of my soul and to move me with terror... It was a sort of slow submarine earthquake which produced strange commotions on the...surface of my life. I was summoned to battle with joy and with fear." Sickness took him to a place where he discovered compassion for himself and others. "[A]s time went on," he wrote, "the peace grew and the terror vanished. It was the peace that was real, and the terror that was an illusion."[8] Sometimes the grace of God shakes our foundations and then we can see clearly like never before.

There is a sense in which we cannot look for grace when we think we have lost it, because we cannot know the form in which grace will come; whether it will be in joy and celebration like Frye's experience early one morning, or in hardship and pain like Didion's. We cannot look for grace, but those who are schooled in these experiences know that this kind of grace looks for us. The most we can say is those epiphanies come at perturbing times and in perturbing worlds. They shake us, in the best sense.

A SIGNAL EVENT

It was a Tuesday like no other. It started out innocently enough. I had overslept. I was due at a meeting with colleagues at the church at 7:30 a.m. I had a quick shower and, forsaking my breakfast, jumped in the car to make my way down the highway from my home to the church. I knew I would arrive a few minutes late, so I put in a call on my cell phone to one of my colleagues, whom I knew would have already arrived for the meeting. He told me the unbelievable news: the World Trade Center was on fire, the Pentagon was on fire, and a plane had crashed in Pennsylvania. I turned on the radio to hear the announcer say that the second tower had just fallen.

When I arrived at the church, the five of us who were supposed to be at the meeting stood around the parking lot in a daze. Then somehow we managed to find ourselves around the board table in the lounge. But we could not start. Everything we were going to talk about, even though it concerned the professional lives of many of our colleagues, seemed now irrelevant and unimportant. I have looked back on that moment many times to try to find a way to describe what was happening as we sat there – silent.

Later, as I emerged from my third meeting and began to prepare for a fourth, my numbness gave way to conviction. I just couldn't do it anymore. I couldn't pretend that it was a normal day. I needed to find something, anything, that made sense on that day of days. And the only thing that made sense was to be with my family. I needed to love and be loved. That's when I cancelled all the other meetings. As Karen Armstrong later wrote, "The events of September 11 were a dark epiphany..."[9] I could see that it was essential to put business aside and connect with loved ones. "To love better," as Emily Dickinson put it.

In March of 1862, the small town of Amherst, Massachusetts, was similarly disabled. The effect of a sudden death on the small community was something like the effect of the 9/11 tragedy on our own hearts and minds. But in Amherst, on that day so long ago, they mourned the loss of a young member of their community to the tragedy of the Civil War. Adjutant Frazer Stearns was 16. He was well-loved. Just a boy. His death numbed the townspeople. Grown men cried in the streets. The poet Emily Dickinson, also a resident of Amherst, worried for the sanity of her older brother, who was wandering around the house wringing his hands saying, "Frazer is dead! Frazer is dead!"

From her own grief she wrote her cousins these words after the funeral: "So our part...is done, but you must come next summer, and we will mind ourselves of this...[soldier] – too brave that he could fear to die. We will play his tunes – maybe he can hear them. We will comfort [his family]." And then, as if Stearns' loss called forth something timeless in us all, Dickinson wrote, "Let us love better, children, it's most that's left to do."[10]

Let us love better.

This same instinct was, I think, reflected poignantly in the faxes, emails, and phone calls that went out to family and colleagues from those inside the World Trade Center after the planes flew into the towers on 9/11. The instinct of many who were in danger, and many who knew they had little time left, was to reassure, to say goodbye, or simply to say, "I love you," to the important people in their lives – before they did anything else.

The same instinct is reflected in the pictures of the lost that were posted on walls near the scene in New York. Invariably, the missing person was pictured with a loved one: a groom with a bride, a mother with a baby, a father with his father. The implication, for all to see, was that while they were at work in the most important economic centre in the world, their hearts were actually with the people they loved most. The pictures say, "This is really who he is; he is a father, a son. She is a mother; she is a daughter – someone who loves and *is* loved. Have you seen her?"

In remembrance of those who died that day, not just in New York but everywhere, we wonder at other losings and other findings – because the days and months and years have given even this horror a little distance.

In 1945, my father was the United Church minister in Claresholm, Alberta. Claresholm was a training base for pilots. As many in the air force will tell you, more pilots were killed during training than were lost overseas. On VE day, 1945, after it was announced that the allies had won the war in Europe, people began to arrive spontaneously and from every direction at the United Church in Claresholm. My father said it was the most incredible thing. Soon the church was full to overflowing with servicemen and townspeople. The most celebratory of worship services then took place – with no preparation, no rehearsals, just an outpouring of gratitude and thanksgiving.

It was the one and only time in my father's 61 years of ministry that he experienced this kind of spontaneous worship and thanksgiving. As I listened to my father tell the story, I marvelled at it. People were more "religious" in those days, I told myself. It seemed impossible that such a thing could happen among those of my own generation.

But 9/11 put the lie to that idea, 56 years after VE day. Not quite spontaneously, but in a matter of hours people who had been strangers just a few days before, both clergy and lay, became united in their desire to organize and gather together for worship. How moving it was that Jews, Lutherans, Roman Catholics, Anglicans, and United Church people were moved in this way. It was as if we had an instinct toward unity so contrary to the culture's impression of us. We were moved more to unity than to division. It was an experience unique in my 30 or so years in the ministry. It was an experience I will never forget.

Only twice in two generations have the churches filled like that. Why? What was the population acknowledging? Was it that our religious institutions have something important to say about peace and war, after all? About consolation and fear, about thanksgiving and uncertainty?

Both VE day and 9/11 drew forth something basic from us: the need to recognize and acknowledge that something larger than ourselves, something significant to all humanity, had happened.

Of course the two events were very different: one was about the end of conflict; about peace, consolation, release, and thanksgiving. The other was about fear, anger, sorrow, uncertainty, and impending war. One celebrated a release that enabled life to move forward; the other acknowledged our sorrow, trepidation, and confusion in the face of a new kind of evil, a thing that might signal the beginning of some end. One was the beginning of a new hope-filled time; the other was the start of a time of profound uncertainty.

But they also have something in common. Times such as these beckon us to pay close attention to the spiritual, to that something hidden and beyond us in which a deep and profound conversation beckons and is necessary in order for us to find our new selves, our hopeful selves, in which the future is lived out. This is particularly important after a deeply disturbing event, such as 9/11, or the Holocaust, which was even more profound. We need to return to these destroyed human landscapes again and again, because every time we do we learn more about ourselves and about what we may do to build a better, more hopeful future together.

It was easy to overestimate the significance of 9/11 just after it happened. About a year later, it seemed to be a rite of passage, a death in our collective life. Not an ordinary death. Not a natural death. It was a murder. Those of us who work with families know that when a murder happens in a family, other dark possibilities may be visited on its coattails. With a natural death, there is a loosening up, a greater acceptance, a willingness to reconcile. It can go dark, too, but for emotionally healthy people who are committed to giving substance to hope, the instinct in the face of a natural death is to love and to regroup, as the first step to healing. A murder, however, a collective murder especially, presents a more formidable challenge.

If we could enter some emotional helicopter that could take us high above these events and the other tragedies of past centuries, what timeless purpose could possibly emerge from these moments? Perhaps only this: that even as the instinct of the emotionally healthy in the face of evil is to connect with loved ones – to love better – the timeless seeks us out and invites us, or we are drawn toward, new purpose. Lost and puzzled as we may be, we may have a sense of being sought out and nudged ever so gently toward something better, even hope.

That alone should sober us enough to listen more than to act, to be silent more than to speak, to let the stirrings of spirit move in us rather than spout convictions, to be found more than to find. Frye insists that there is timeless meaning even in the most heinous events.[11] He also says that it is the task of the faithful community to attempt to articulate a vision even out of the ashes. All historical events are out of our range once they have happened; "it is only the verbal event that concerns us, and the verbal event may be the starting point of an adventure in understanding."[12]

Naturally, a collective dejection settled over North America after 9/11. I hardly need to catalogue what happened. It is well-known. We talked ourselves into a recession. Those community functions that call forth the good in the human spirit – symphonies, theatres, and art galleries – reported a sharp downturn in attendance. So many people, in what leisure time they had, turned on the television and became mesmerized by announcements of security levels and anthrax scares.

My children and I went trick-or-treating the Halloween night after September 11 and we made a point of calling on a household we knew just around the corner. And as we neared the house, I could see the incandescent light of the television dancing off the walls in the darkness. And as they put treats into my children's sacks, our friends spoke absent-mindedly about their obsession with the news and their feelings of confusion. These were educated people.

How interesting that our collective instinct was to shut off all but the input of CNN, which had the effect of mesmerizing us further. We shut out or put away the best of our culture. Things might have been so much better had we read Jane Austen, listened to Mozart, re-read some favourite poetry, gone to the theatre or to a concert. We might have fared so much better, emotionally and spiritually, had we done something to help awaken what Harold Bloom calls the desire to be simpler, to be more truthful, to be more human, to be more ourselves. Some people found that attending synagogue, mosque, or church helped switch on the part of themselves that is not isolated but thrives in the company of others. When we engage with the best and the most worthy in human culture, Bloom adds, a miracle takes place. When we search for ourselves in the best of our culture, we prepare ourselves for change. It gets us on our feet and moving. Like a boxer dancing, it readies us for challenge.

But what is the challenge? When those proponents of a new darkness threaten, we owe it to ourselves, our souls, our bodies – and to the souls and bodies of our children and their children – to fight every darkness as it threatens the human heart. We owe it to ourselves to search for and follow that small shining star of hope amid the darkness of our times, as did the wise men in Matthew's narrative. This calls for extraordinary measures far more than revenge.

In Shakespeare's *Measure for Measure*, Isabella brings her accusation against her tormenter, Angelo, who sought to seduce her in return for sparing her brother's life, but betrayed her by seducing her (he thinks) and ordering her brother's execution anyway. After his treachery is exposed, Angelo is ordered to marry his betrothed,

Mariana, and then face execution. In desperation, Mariana pleads with Isabella to forgive him. This forgiveness would save his life. Remarkably, Isabella not only agrees to forgive him, but actually pleads for his life.

In a remarkable statement on the scene, Frye says of Isabella's actions, "if one's essential humanity can be made to speak, even once in one's life, one has a centre to revolve around ever after."[13] September 11 was one example of the kind of moment that invites us to act as Isabella acted, that invites us to speak the kind of word she speaks, that invites us to forgiveness and toward something bold and unexpected. It's about speaking – despite all contrary emotions – the language of love, as we shall see.

A SIGNAL RESPONSE

If you blame it on the barbarians, then you
are saying it has nothing to do with us.
– Iain Pears, "Barbarians Within"[14]

Most people are familiar with the names and the events: Auschwitz, Hiroshima, Gandhi, Kennedy, Martin Luther King Jr., Vietnam, 9/11, the tsunamis of 2004 and 2011, and others. Events such as these have the power to cause an emotional shift.

As humans, we need hope, which is not exactly the same thing as optimism, as Desmond Tutu noted when he stopped David Frost mid-interview to say he was not an optimist. Optimism suggests that everything is "okay" and will stay that way. Don't worry, be happy! Hope is something deeper, more profound, more an expression of the universal spirit. Hope is a mandate; it believes in the possibility that things will be better some day in the future, no matter how dark or ominous things are in the present.

Hope, in buoyant times, has its own momentum for breeding more hope. But this buoyancy can leave us following times of darkness and crisis, whether it's a personal crisis or a communal crisis. In these times, we are called to redirect our hope.

I am convinced that after such events, personal or corporate, there is much we can do to avert more calamity and more disaster in our hearts and minds. We may direct our hope differently.

In one of Jesus' parables, the principal character is faced with a crisis. It is more personal, but his response to the crisis is instructive to that situation. Let's look at the story, which is told in Luke 16:1–13.[15]

A dishonest manager works for a decent, hardworking and very wealthy landlord. For some time, the manager has been under suspicion for corruption. Eventually, the landlord finds conclusive evidence that the manager is dishonest and dismisses him.

Rather than protest his innocence, the manager remains silent. His silence is an admission of guilt. He knows there is nothing he can say. He is guilty. The landlord has every right now to have him thrown in jail. In fact, the crowd listening to Jesus tell the parable will expect that this is the fate of such a dishonest manager. But, contrary to local custom, the landlord lets him go. This is absolutely shocking. Unheard of. Never done.

The dishonest manager is overwhelmed by the landlord's mercy. But he knows that, even though he has not gone to jail, his very survival is at stake. When word gets out that he was dismissed and why, he will be unable to find employment in the community.

As if buoyed by the forgiveness of the landlord, the manager casts off all fear and decides the only way he will be able to survive in the community after this disaster is to call upon the landlord's mercy once more. He says to himself, "If the landlord was merciful once, he will be merciful again!" He knows that mercy resides in the landlord's heart, like a deep bottomless pool. So before word of his dismissal gets out, he goes to those who are in debt to the landlord and tells them that their debts have been reduced!

Well, the debtors think that the manager has convinced the landlord to have mercy on *them*. All of a sudden, the manager and the landlord are heroes in the community. There is dancing in the streets, feasting. Everyone is discussing with one another the virtues of the manager and the landlord. The manager has secured for himself a place in the community.

The news of the celebrating gets back to the landlord. He is in a real bind. At first he is furious! That scoundrel has cheated him out of his rightful debt revenue. But what can he do? He can't tell his tenants the manager was speaking out of turn. They would brand him a cheapskate at best and double-crosser at worst. He decides it would be better not to say anything at all.

See, the landlord knows he's now the hero of the village. What else can he do, but praise the manager for his shrewdness? In fact, after the landlord thinks awhile, he has a kind of admiration for the manager. He praises him for his powers of self-preservation. I imagine that he himself must have been forgiven at some point in time. Forgiveness begets forgiveness in human community. Otherwise, how could he have such forgiveness in him?

But why would Jesus tell this story at all? Why would he make the hero of this amazing story a dishonest man? Because, for Jesus, the pressing issue here is not the manager's virtue, but the power of mercy to promote health in a community, and one person's ability to recognize crisis and personal failure as an opportunity to bring evidence of the power of mercy much closer to his own consciousness and to the consciousness of his community.

To return to the example of 9/11, one thing it did was bring Islam closer to public consciousness. As a clergyperson in a liberal Protestant denomination at the time, I was suddenly very aware of my ignorance of what my Muslim brothers and sisters actually believed. It seemed that the calamity of this event in history was calling me, in the face of our collective fear, to the same kind of strategizing the dishonest manager displayed. Crisis always calls the spiritual person to refocus their hope, to find some opportunity in tragedy.

On a local level, I was forced to ask what our Muslim neighbours would expect from the likes of the non-Muslims in our community. In their fear and ours, they would expect to feel our hostility more than ever. But what if we offered friendship instead? What if we took the initiative to learn more about Islam? What if we were to learn more about their customs and values? What if the churches, spiritual centres of the community, led the way on this? What if we were to offer our Muslim brothers and sisters our hospitality? Could something good come out of this unspeakable outrage, I wondered?

The answer is as simple as it is counter-intuitive. I believe, with Jesus, in the imminence of mercy and its ability to communicate the language of love. That belief calls me to act differently when times change, not to cease hoping but instead to seek hope in new directions.

At its very core, Jesus' message is not about goodness and badness so much as it is about how to be healthy in community, especially in extreme circumstances. How do we foster health within the communities in which we live and work?

A senior clergy colleague of mine was gravely ill. He was one of the saints of the church in the city in which he lived and worked his whole life. And he was so brave. I know that because another colleague of his told me that he went to see him just a few days before he died. This colleague was at a loss. He told his very sick friend that he didn't know what to say to him or what to do. All his words were empty, it seemed. He just stammered in the presence of death and then fell silent. On his sick bed, his grateful colleague said, "You know, miracles are sometimes found in recovery from sickness, but the miraculous is always found in the bond of friendship. You are my friend. Just hold my hand awhile."

Jesus' parable points at our hearts. Jesus' parable points us toward the future, toward a new day. It is a new day that requires new initiatives, new approaches to love. An epiphany has happened. What is our view? How will we respond?

The parable shows us a person – like us, not a paragon of virtue – who experiences mercy and who believes in that mercy so strongly it helps him out of his own self-victimization, all because he has learned to trust in that immanent power. I think we are called to do the same, to live that most difficult of difficult things. To love mercy. To expect mercy. To give mercy.

FREEDOM, SUBSTANCE, AND HOPE

Now faith is the substance of things hoped for,
the assurance of things not seen.
– Hebrews 11:1, KJV (alt.)

Not long ago, I was talking to a girl in Grade 2 or 3 and she was reliving the terrible experience of her first math test. It wasn't just any math test, but a timed math test. I remember those tests well. Sweaty palms. Hands sticking to the paper. In the absence of memory, praying to

God for a right answer, as if God cared. And all the while, the child next to you is busily writing and perhaps even humming to herself.

The little girl telling me about her experience looked at me. There were tears in her eyes; her face was a little pale. In a voice full of quiet desperation, she said, "I thought my head was going to explode." Sometimes change is like that.

There is a story about Jesus and ten lepers (Luke 17:11–19), one of whom thinks his head is going to explode. Nine of the lepers are Jews; the tenth is Samaritan. Of course, Jews and Samaritans were bitter enemies and would never travel together unless they were joined or unified by the defilement of sickness. Sick people, even those with minor skin ailments, were banished to the tombs on the edge of the villages, just to be sure. They were like our homeless people today – unlikely travel companions joined by misfortune.

The ten lepers call out to Jesus from a distance. Jesus tells them to go and show themselves to the priests at the temple in Jerusalem. The moment the lepers turn their backs on Jesus and head to Jerusalem, they are cured. Let's leave the miracle bit aside. But hold on a minute. There is something terribly wrong with one part of this picture. The Samaritan man was also heading to Jerusalem and to the priests at the temple. He was unlikely to get a welcome reception there. Once the other nine lepers had been found to be clean by the priests, they would have been bathed by the priests in the waters of purification and so would have been able to re-enter the community as full participants. But not so the tenth leper.

As already mentioned, Jews had no dealings with Samaritans. And Samaritans did not recognize Jerusalem as a holy city, nor its priests as holy people. In fact, Samaritans despised Jerusalem. They despised the priests. Only a few years before, some Samaritans had defiled the temple in Jerusalem during Passover by scattering human bones in the temple court. Talk about civil disobedience!

In other words, for the tenth leper to enter Jerusalem and the temple would have gone against the grain. To go to Jerusalem would have been to turn himself inside out, to turn against his own people and his own traditions. More than that, it would have been dangerous. The priests would have seen by his dress that he was not a Jew. Everyone would have known. He might even have been set upon or killed before he reached the temple, or Jerusalem for that matter.

Still, the tenth leper, the Samaritan, decided to walk. Despite all logic or thoughts for his own safety, despite all appearances and every tradition, he decided that this Jesus of Nazareth was trustworthy.

In other words, the tenth leper displayed the kind of faith the writer of Hebrews had in mind – the substance of things hoped for. The tenth leper found substance in his hoping and was assured by it.

This is a wonderful definition of faith, but it is an even better definition of spiritual freedom as Frye understood it. Frye says that such a vision is an imaginative one, meaning not that it is a kind of illusion, as Freud argued, but that it is a story we enter into and in that story we find something truly extraordinary – a superlative and overarching kind of freedom.[16]

For those who are put off by the word faith because of the implied necessity of a deity, perhaps the word freedom can be inserted in its place. There is a freedom to be found in placing to one side the logic or "the usual way" that we face all the time. In the leper's case, those constraints stood in the way of healing and told him he could not find healing as a Samaritan amongst Jews. Yet he found freedom in the substantive, visionary hope that his religion did not matter. Or, more to the point, his religion derived from one realm of concern, but his freedom from something else entirely.

At that instant, when he found himself cured with the others, he suddenly didn't need to go to Jerusalem because he had already been there in his few short steps toward it, in his willingness – and with a remarkable lack of constraint – to go toward the culturally and religiously impossible. He was willing to go into a "story" that is, as Emily Dickinson might have said it, at slant to the accustomed narrative he had been raised in.

This need not be a religious notion for us anymore than it was for the Samaritan. Religion has no franchise on this kind of freedom. Religious faith can be a kind of portal into this imaginative way of being free, but this kind of freedom is not contingent on it. It's just as likely that something else may trip us into it and then once we are in it and live in it awhile, we may find ourselves getting accustomed to it as a way of being. Then it may become a kind of practice, a sort of habit.

When he realizes that he has been cured, the tenth leper comes back to Jesus straight away to give thanks. For he had been nobody, literally, and now he is somebody. On a figurative level, he left the literal behind and embraced the spiritual. He had been chained in so many ways and now he is free, all because he was willing to experiment with a radical and profound difference, which for the biblical writer was Jesus himself.

Of course, it is not a blind difference, as the writer of Hebrews implies. The tenth leper has a sense that there is substance in pursuing this hope. Sometimes the freedom we find at these crossroads moments calls us to do something different, something we have never done before, something uncharacteristic. As we move into that giving-substance-to-hope, we may find ourselves in unfamiliar territory, travelling an uncertain road with a doubtful destination. But in walking that uncertain and doubtful road, even just by heading in that direction, and despite the fact that our head feels like it is going to explode, something new about ourselves and about how hope impinges on our lives is revealed to us.

Remember that famous scene in *The Miracle Worker*, where Anne Sullivan, Helen Keller's teacher, is trying to bring the young Helen out of her dark isolation? Helen can't see and she can't hear. Helen and Anne are at the water pump. Anne douses Helen with water and despite Helen's resistance is able to forge or suggest a link in Helen's mind between what Helen feels – the water – and a word spelled out in sign language in her hand. Through that terrible effort, a new world is opened up for Helen. It was a kind of baptism, I guess. Helen was able to give substance to a hope she didn't know she had – then becomes one of the most powerful witnesses to hope of her generation. An explosion of hope preceded by an implosion of resistance. That's how it works.

Many years ago, a couple I knew was experiencing marital problems. Both were very close to me and their relationship very important to our friendship, and yet I was helpless to do anything. It seemed as the weeks and months wore on that they were sliding down some slippery slope no one could control. And then came a kind of breakthrough.

The woman told me that her therapist had advised her to stop concentrating on repairing the relationship, which didn't seem to be working. The therapist advised her to set her own goals, to make substantial her own hope for herself.

This woman had sacrificed everything for her marriage and her family over a number of years. But she took those first steps toward substantive hope and, all of a sudden, as the husband noticed differences in her, he too began to set goals for himself. The effect was to set that couple on a new road for their relationship. It could have gone either way, but hope in crisis is often like that. We are moved toward difference, and sometimes even through the dissolution of the old, a better way is to be found.

Of course, the crisis or instigating event could be any one of a number of things. We get a diagnosis; we hear tragic news; our life is turned upside down. We are forced onto that bitter road to Jerusalem like the leper; we feel that our head might explode. And then on the road we see little bits of light through the cracks in the darkness.

We cannot go back to where we were before, but if we believe there is some purpose for us in this life, freedom beckons to us and urges us forward. We believe there is a way forward. Perhaps like the wise men who followed the star, we will travel forward, or find "home," by a different way, a different route, a way we might have resisted before the changing event. But freedom in a way, is directing us. We realize that we cannot let ourselves be crippled by fear, but only move toward the new. What will we do differently? Because this is now a different time and requires different behaviour that will give substance to new hope.

Epiphanies tend to be like that.

THE LANGUAGE OF LOVE

[I]n the New Testament love is regarded not as one virtue among others but the only virtue there is.
– Northrop Frye, *Complete Works*[17]

Richard Nixon once said, "It is fear that motivates people, not love. They don't tell you that in Sunday school, but it's true." Actually, he may have been right, at least in *his* universe. But hopeful people don't talk about motivation in the same way. They don't talk about what naturally drives a person to do things, because they don't believe that the obvious or even practiced way is necessarily the best way. Nixon didn't get that.

Hope demands that we obey the commands of a different universe – an alternative universe, if you will – to the one we've been handed. Hopeful people aim in the direction of love, even though we may not really get there and though we may fall woefully short of the ultimate goal. We are like tennis players on the professional circuit. We need to practice to get to the top. But many of us never get there. It doesn't matter. The striving is everything.

The Bible gives us many creeds to live by, many formal statements that may help us, but no creedal statement is more helpful, more able to help us with the boundary between fear (the natural motivator), and love or agape (the hopeful motivator), than Paul's love poem in 1 Corinthians 13:1–13. Frye takes the apostle Paul at his word and finds in this passage the kind of freedom we may live *by* and *in*.[18] Here is an excerpt from the *Revised English Bible*.

Love is patient and kind. Love envies no one,
is never boastful, never conceited, never rude;
love is never selfish, never quick to take offence.
Love keeps no score of wrongs, takes no pleasure
in the sins of others, but delights in the truth.
There is nothing love cannot face; there is no

limit to its faith, its hope, its endurance.
Love will never come to an end... At present we
see only puzzling reflections in a mirror, but one
day we shall see face to face. My knowledge now
is partial; then it will be whole... There are three
things that last forever: faith, hope, and love;
and the greatest of the three is love.

This is a creedal statement for the entire human community. I heard it read not long ago at a man's celebration of life service after he died. Hearing it and knowing the man as I did, I could see how he fulfilled the ideals of the passage on love. Hearing it read, we who were there to honour him could find strength from his witness and could recommit ourselves to the same quest ourselves. That's what happens when we read prophetic poetry in the context of community. And, by the way, God is not mentioned in the passage at all except in passing.

Notice that the passage tells us not only what *not* to do, but what we *may* do. We may be patient and kind. We may leave envy behind. We may be large of heart rather than possessive. We don't have to insist on our own way. Though absolute "truth" may not be available to us in spiritual matters, as Frye reminds us,[19] only reflections in a darkened mirror, these are things we may sink our hearts into. This is a direction in which we may head. These things are doable, even if not absolutely achievable.

Moreover – and this is very bold of Paul – he goes so far as to say that this love, of all human activity, has a pre-eminent timeless quality. In other words, the creativity that springs from this practice and our attempts to achieve love pass from generation to generation doing good until the very last day! It's about creating and maintaining healthy human community. Again, it is about the timeless.

And here is another aspect to the timeless part. This language, the language of love, Frye argues,[20] is the same language spoken by God. What are the implications of this? It means that in this love activity we have a window on the nature of God. That God is patient and kind. That God is not envious. That God has a largeness of heart. That God is not possessive. That God does not insist on God's own way. I am tempted to equate God with freedom, as Frye understands freedom – a vision of the spiritual life that continues to transform and expand our own.

It is about what the human community may achieve: health rather than hate; healing rather than festering woundedness; courage rather than fear – our world rendered healthy, our children healthy, and our children's children healthy. In the here and now, in this world, in this time, in this place! It may be done if we can find it in our hearts to speak consistently, or even head in the direction of love.

Paul sets out in his love poem the possibility for us to be self-critical. The question is not whether the country is going to hell in a handbasket, but how can I be a better citizen in this country? The question is not how the family can be better for me, but how can I be better for the family; not how can I get my children to treat me better, but how can I be a better parent for my children; a better partner, a better sister, a better child? In other words, in this love universe, it's not about the other guy and their deficits; it's about me and my effort to create surplus. I don't know about you, but this is a universe I don't know very well. And I'd like to get to know it better.

Epiphanies do that for us. They invite us into that difference.

One cold December morning not long ago, my mother's sister died at the age of 103. Ruth was an amazing person: admired by her children, a favourite with all her nieces and nephews, revered by all in her small community. She was active in her church, but somehow she rose above the boundaries of all parts of that community. The night before she died, a group from the local Catholic church came in to sing her favourite Christmas carol.

On the very same morning she died, at The Patch, a vintage clothing store in Victoria some 12 hours' journey from her town, Bronwyn, my youngest child, was working the morning shift. It had been an unusually cold December in the Pacific Northwest. The homeless were in a particularly dire situation. That day nine homeless people died of Fentanyl poisoning in Vancouver's Downtown Eastside.

A very old lady came into the store, walked up to Bronwyn as if they were friends, and asked to be given a sweater. Bronwyn could see that this woman looked particularly dishevelled and thin, and noticed that she had sores on her face. Giving away clothes was strictly against store policy, but Bronwyn went off to the manager to plead the woman's cause. The manager relented and they gave her not only a sweater, but a toque and scarf as well. The woman seemed very pleased.

After the woman left the store, Bronwyn came up with the idea of making an opportunity for patrons to contribute to a fund for homeless people in the Victoria area. When Bronwyn told me the story and what they had done because of the visit of the old woman, I said, "Honey, that was an angel." Bronwyn was dubious. But I was sure. What I didn't say was that Bronwyn was channelling the spirit of my mother's sister, who would have done exactly the same.

Who knows what is factually true, but truth cannot be known in spiritual matters, only in metaphor and myth, as Frye argued. There was a freedom present in the dilemma Bronwyn faced – a freedom not found in the limitations of the situation, but in the opportunity the epiphany afforded.

NOTES

1. Frye, *Collected Works*, 305. See also, *Double Vision*, 20, 76.
2. Frye, *Double Vision*, 14–21.
3. This incident was related by Northrop Frye to a reporter in 1981 in an article in one of the weekly magazines (likely the *Star Weekly*), which came with the Saturday newspaper in those days.
4. John Dominic Crossan, *In Parables: The Challenge of the Historical Jesus* (New York: Harper & Row, 1973). Crossan's book has been most helpful to me in understanding this concept. Consider for example Matthew 2:2–16. Northrop Frye makes this point repeatedly as the very nature of prophecy itself.
5. Joan Didion, *The Year of Magical Thinking* (New York: Vintage Books, 2005), 74–75.
6. Ibid., 75.
7. Quoted in *Flannery O'Connor*, ed. Harold Bloom (New York: Infobase Publishing, 2009), 18. This book was part of the series "Bloom's Modern Critical Reviews."
8. Thomas Merton, *The Sign of Jonas* (New York: Houghton Mifflin Harcourt, 2002), 231.
9. Karen Armstrong, *The Spiral Staircase: My Climb Out of Darkness* (New York: Alfred A. Knopf, 2004), 303.
10. Richard B. Sewall, *The Life of Emily Dickinson* (New York: Farrar, Straus and Giroux, 1974), 640.
11. Frye, *Collected Works*, 278.
12. Frye, *Double Vision*, 76.
13. Frye, *Collected Works*, 152.

14. Quoted in Sandra Martin, "Barbarians Within," *Globe and Mail*, July 29, 2002, updated April 17, 2008.

15. The analysis that follows is taken from Kenneth Bailey, *Poet and Peasant: A Literary Cultural Approach to the Parables in Luke* (Grand Rapids: Eerdmans, 1976), 86–118.

16. Frye, *Double Vision*, 19.

17. Frye, *Collected Works*, 164.

18. Frye, *Double Vision*, 17–18.

19. Ibid., 20

20. Ibid., 21.

LENT

[T]he death of Christ on the cross
makes it possible for a [person] to see a few
other things besides hell.
– Northrop Frye, *Collected Works*[1]

LENT, THE 40 DAYS BEFORE EASTER, is the second great penitential season in the Christian year, the first one being Advent. For many people, Lent has been understood as a time to give up things, as a purgative of sorts.

It reminds me of something my paternal grandmother used to do. My grandmother had a great cure for what she called biliousness. She would take Epsom salts. The idea was that she would ream out her system so that it could start over again. Many of us who inherited some of her genes have since discovered that we have a slight intolerance to dairy products and that if we get bilious we just need to go off dairy for a while, or take a pill with the lactase enzyme in it. It's a less drastic kind of action, let me assure you.

In Western culture, we harbour certain beliefs about purgatives. For example, we used to practice bloodletting, in which blood was drained from a patient in an effort to balance the body's humours (fluids) and thereby increase health. Unfortunately, the practice often weakened patients, sometimes to the point that it killed not just the disease, but the patient as well.

The second generation in my family did not rely on Epsom salts except to soak their feet, thank goodness. But I do seem to recall some trauma around the "e" word. My mother, usually a very gentle woman, would suddenly get very aggressive with me around the "e" word. I have no idea what my symptoms might have been, but I recall the bathroom door shut and locked, her hot water bottle hanging from the bathrobe hook at the back of the door, a contraption with a rubber hose and metal clamps attached to it, and my mother bending me over her knee – the only time she ever did that. It was awful! But was it good for me?

Family histories aside, the idea of giving things up for Lent as a purgative has never really caught on in the mainline Protestant imagination, which is perhaps a good thing. Northrop Frye has pointed out that the practice of giving things up for Lent goes back a long way, to a time long before the Christian era.[2] In fact, it stretches back to the time when our early forebears began to sow seeds in spring. Lent is actually an Old English word for spring, and the practice of renunciation reflects our ancestors' anxieties about seeds sprouting. Will they sprout or not? How can we help that happen? What if we starve ourselves, abstain from sex, or engage in some kind of purging? If we deprive ourselves of something we enjoy, maybe that will help the seeds grow. Magical thinking, to be sure. A collective kind of obsessive-compulsive disorder.

But Lent is so much more, or rather, Lent is something else altogether.

RETREAT INTO LEISURE

One of the finest theological minds of the 20th century was a young man by the name of Dietrich Bonhoeffer. In 1943, he was arrested by the Gestapo for conspiring to assassinate Adolph Hitler. Two years later he was executed even as the Allied artillery could be heard in the distance. He had produced some great work before his imprisonment, but his time in prison became a rich period of theological reflection and a powerful witness to the present day.

Early in his imprisonment, Bonhoeffer wrote to his parents: "The great thing is to stick to what one still has and can do – there is still plenty left – and not to be dominated by the thought of what one cannot do, and by feelings of resentment and discontent."[3] That's quite a statement by someone in prison and under threat of execution.

Later, Bonhoeffer states that this is the true biblical meaning of temptation. He says, "Quite suddenly" one's heart becomes "deceitful above all things," as if one's own best energy for good is somehow reversed and enlisted into battle against us. This is different than what we usually think of as temptation: as a little devil sitting on our shoulder whispering in our ear; or as Leonard Cohen has written, various forms of "Hey, why not ask for more?"[4] Temptation is not that nasty little voice. Rather, it is an engine inside of us that drives our best selves, but put in reverse and used to convince us that we are no good at all.

Put another way, let's assume that there is an ongoing purpose for each one of us in each stage of our life's journey, in each day on our way, in each moment of that day. When we let ourselves listen to the voice that speaks of our own futility, we have heard and yielded to the voice of temptation. In other words, temptation is less a defect of the will and more a refusal to believe in what we can be for the world.

The primary biblical reading for Lent is the scene in three of the gospels where Jesus is tempted by Satan, one of the few moments when the "fallen one" actually makes an appearance in the Christian part of the Bible. That appearance has misled us.

In truth, as Bonhoeffer suggested, it was Jesus' own extraordinary drive to be entirely for others that was put into reverse and enlisted to convince him that he could, if he chose, be the opposite; he could be a person entirely for himself. This was the temptation Jesus faced in the wilderness.[5]

Our own temptation is like Jesus' temptation. When we say, "Lead us not into temptation" during the Lord's Prayer, we repeat what Jesus entreated us to say: Let not my strong powers for constructive good and the accompanying momentum for constructive good that is given me be reversed in my own mind and heart and used against me so that I come to think that I can do no good at all, except for myself.

So Lent isn't a time to confess our peccadilloes or to give up things. Lent is a time to recommit ourselves and to get clearer in our minds about our purpose on this earth. And, if we think we don't *have* a purpose, we need to think again and discover it, or rediscover it, lest other powers be enlisted to defeat us.

A number of years ago, HBO came out with a series called *Six Feet Under*. Once I read the early rave reviews, I started watching. I was fascinated that Hollywood would actually be interested in the lives of funeral directors, whose encounters with people overlap those of clergy, at least to some degree. Ultimately, I was disappointed, although I stuck with the show through all five seasons. I was disappointed for a whole range of reasons: the usual misrepresentation of the church and religion in all its forms, and the usual preoccupation of Hollywood with sex, primarily. These were very messed up and unhappy characters.

Yet as screwed up as the characters were and in spite of myself, I began to care about them. What was most interesting, though, was a technique used by Allan Ball, the creator of the series, in which the dead visited the living. Sometimes they would visit in a dream, sometimes in a daydream, sometimes in a reflective moment. And sometimes the dead would say what they might have said if they had still been living. Usually they said helpful things, but sometimes they would be the negative voices of the characters themselves incarnated in the dead person. I'm sure Ball didn't know it, but in these negative voices he actually captures the biblical notion of temptation, according to Bonhoeffer.

In the second last year of the series, David – one of the adult children in the family who form the principals in the series – has an extremely violent encounter with a hitchhiker. David is gay and throughout the series had struggled with his sexual identity. The attack is emphatically anti-gay and recalled real attacks on gay men in rural America at the time.

Even though he survives it, the attack continues to haunt David. Even though the attacker ends up in prison, he revisits David repeatedly in random dreams, especially after the death of someone very close to David. Thankfully, for those of us who toughed it out to the end, in the final episode David is able to summon his inner strength and talk back to the negative voices. He is able to say, "You don't exist!" And then he actually attacks the image, only to discover that under the hood obscuring the face of the attacker is his own face, the face of his frightened self, which he then hugs.

In other words, David is able to say out loud, and to act out, "lead me not into temptation," according to Bonhoeffer's definition. It turns his life around. In the next scene, he begins to pray for the first time in the series; he says grace at the dinner table and thanks God for his young family.

Interesting isn't it? The gestalt David uses – talking out loud to the tempter – is biblical too. Jesus himself spoke out loud to his tempter, to what we would now call that nagging inner voice. It's a practice I recommend. When you are in the shower or are getting ready for the day and you start having negative thoughts about what you can do, when you start putting yourself down – which is the proper meaning of "temptation" in the biblical sense – I heartily recommend saying out loud, "Go away!" or "You don't exist!" It works, though you might want to do it when no one else is around, in case they get the wrong impression.

Simone Weil said Lent is about "paying close attention," and I think that too is the way forward. Certainly, the way forward for Jesus was to pay close attention to what he was about, what God intended for him. He knew, or perhaps he came to know through experience, that he was properly a person for others and not a person for himself.

Frye noted that Milton, in his wonderful poem *Paradise Regained*, shows that in the temptation in the wilderness, Jesus "clarifies his mind about his mission as the Messiah." In other words, in the agony of his separation from his Abba (father), Jesus finds himself and discovers his true mission. He discovers what Abba wants him to do.[6]

Frye also observed that the better word for the appropriate activity in the season of Lent is "leisure" rather than "denial." That idea may seem counterintuitive, but Frye means leisure not in the sense of laziness or inactivity, but as "a period of total concentration on the work of the mind."[7]

In Lent, we are invited to detach our minds from action. It is a kind of Sabbath or sabbatical period. Those who have taken a sabbatical or who have struggled to keep Sabbath know it is easier said than done. We are besought on every side by voices that urge banality, guilt, brooding, and worry upon us. The whole point of Lent is to separate ourselves from those voices and to be assured of our purpose. Lent, Frye insists, is properly a leisure spent quieting down the conflict of impulses; of getting all forms of awareness – intellectual, emotional, sensual, imaginative – to work together instead of trying to seize control of the will.[8]

Another way to say it is that in Lent we should become "students" of ourselves, full of curiosity about ourselves, wondering what motivates us and how. Lent invites us to question what we have come to assume about ourselves, and to arrive at new understandings of why we chose the old ones in the first place.

I love to follow the human interest stories that arise from great sporting events such as the Olympics. In 2002, Canadians followed closely the drama of Jamie Salé and David Pelletier, the Canadian figure skaters at the heart of the Olympic scandal in pairs skating at Salt Lake City. Salé and Pelletier were deprived of what everyone except the judges agreed was a gold-medal performance. Eventually, after an extraordinary about-face by the judges, Salé and Pelletier ended up sharing the gold medal with the other team. But before that happened, I watched their news conference the day after they won only the silver medal. How impressive they were! At one point, when pressed by a reporter to declare if they would now turn professional, Salé said, "We never make a decision on a high or a low; we just let it all sink in for a while and then we decide."

Let the spirit drive you into the wilderness. Be a student of the leisure of reflectiveness. Find your freedom there.

A colleague told me about a woman he knew whose spouse had died the previous year. She spent Lent that year writing in a journal about her experience of being alone after 25 years of marriage. Then she sent the journal to friends in various parts of the country. Her friends, in turn, wrote responses in her journal to what she had written, and then sent it back to her. For the woman, it was a wonderful way to concentrate her mind on the task at hand – the need to deal with her grief. In the process, she not only honoured her relationship with her husband, she honoured the friendships she had so valued over the years, and these friends honoured her. The exercise helped her reach a point where she could once again look forward in time, not just backwards. It was a time of leisure in the best sense.

Have you ever dwelt on a complicated issue – something related to your life purpose perhaps – and become totally stymied? When you've reached that point, have you ever gone out and dug in the earth, or watched the birds, or breathed the air of a green forest and then come back to the problem? If you have, you'll know that quite often the problem figuratively flips over on its back for you. You come back with a new perspective or insight or awareness, and everything shifts. This is not flaky stuff. It's about a relationship we have that we often neglect – our vital relationship with ourselves.

Iris Murdoch wrote these lines: "I am looking out of my window in an anxious and resentful state of mind, brooding perhaps on some damage done to my prestige. Then suddenly I observe a hovering kestrel. And when I return to thinking of the other matter it seems less important… we take a self-forgetful pleasure in the sheer alien pointless independent existence of animals, birds, stones and trees."[9] And in them we may find ourselves again.

My colleague in ministry, Gerald van Wyck, told me one day that he had tickets to see Cecilia Bartoli, the great mezzo-soprano. Cora, Gerry's wife, was attending a workshop and couldn't go. I tripped over the words, "I'll go with you!" I was thrilled. I didn't know much about Bertoli or her music, but I had seen her picture and, well, never look a gift ticket in the mouth. That was on Thursday. By Saturday at 4:00, I was less than enthusiastic. My sermon prep had not gone well and I half hoped Gerry wouldn't call. But he did call and we went. It turned out to be the musical event of my life-time. The next day, some in my congregation said the sermon was the best I had ever preached. Should I have been surprised? Not really. When you notice the beautiful around you and thereby get some distance from whatever you're struggling with, you almost inevitably find yourself paying closer attention to your life purpose – the act of leisure.

Lent is a time to pay close attention. It is a time to concentrate our minds on what really matters – our life's purpose. It is a time to clear away the negative voices that try to defeat us, and the debris from those voices. This is what Dietrich Bonhoeffer saw so clearly in that Nazi prison, knowing full well that he was, in all likelihood, a dead man walking.

THE LIONESS AND THE ORYX

A few years back, a Kenyan lioness was perplexing wild-life experts.[10] At first, they thought it was a fluke when she adopted an oryx calf. But then, after the first adopted antelope was eaten by a more orthodox lioness, it happened again – on Valentine's Day no less. The same lioness adopted another oryx calf. Game wardens said the lioness spent a day lying down with the delicate calf in the shade of an acacia tree, grooming it and warding off predators. The lioness had nursed her first baby antelope for two weeks, nudging it gently across the savannah, and had been seen following oryx herds ever since. The story certainly gives new meaning to the biblical vision of the lamb and the lion lying down together. Perhaps the lioness was born again in some way.

But I must not play fast and loose with a term that is very important to some Christians. Perhaps I should attempt to explain what I mean by the term "born again," if only to clarify the nonsense I seem to be writing. For some people, the term "born again" refers to a specific time and place when, motivated by the spirit, they gave their life over to Jesus. Some of those people might describe it as the first moment of the rest of their life.

John Wesley, the English cleric who co-founded Methodism, famously reported in his own diary that there was a moment one night in a meeting at Aldersgate, London, when his heart was "strangely warmed." It happened to St. Paul too, on the road to Damascus. He was blinded and heard Jesus speaking. But is this what Jesus means when he speaks of being "born again" (John 3:1–17)?

The phrase originates in the King James Version of the Bible. It is uttered by Jesus when Nicodemus, a member of the governing council of the Jews, wants to give Jesus a fair hearing. Nicodemus is attracted by the message of Jesus so he goes to Jesus at night, under cover of darkness, as if, even while dwelling in his own dark-but-comfortable tomb, he has a sense that there might be more, and that Jesus might actually deliver more.

In the original Greek text, Jesus doesn't use the phrase "born again" at all. He says no one can experience the kingdom of God without being born "from above," which is perhaps even more cryptic. "No one can enter the kingdom of God without being born of water and spirit [*pneuma*] ... The wind [*pneuma*] blows where it wills; you hear the sound of it, but you do not know where it comes from or where it is going. So it is with everyone born of the spirit [*pneuma*]." (John 3:3, 5–7). In Greek, the word *pneuma* can refer to either spirit or wind. Translators have used "spirit" for *pneuma* when it suits them, and "wind" at other points. Frye wants none of it. He wants wind used throughout the passage.

What does it mean? Frye saw it this way: Think of the power of water and wind in our world – the havoc they create – the impossibility of controlling them in any absolute way. The phrase, then, can only refer to freedom. "Born from above" seems to suggest that, for Jesus, without God the world is like an underground realm of roots and constraints and darkness – the world of the earth worm, which is fine for earth worms, but not great for humans. And then there is another world above ground, as it were. "Above is a daylight world of space and colour...where clear water flows and air blows freely."[11] In other words, we can choose to live in the world constrained by all sorts of things, like an earth worm, and or we can choose to live freely, like the wind and water.

Another event from the 2002 Winter Olympics comes to mind. Sarah Hughes, the American figure skater, was an example of someone who lived with this kind of spirit. She was 16 years old when she went out on the ice one Thursday night and won the gold medal against all odds. What was the difference between her attitude and the attitude of the favourites in her event, fellow American Michelle Kwan, and Russian Irina Slutskaya?

The difference, it seems, was very simple. Sarah Hughes was just glad to be there. She had nothing to lose and everything to win, so she went out there, she said, and had fun! Her competitors were constrained by the pressure and you could see it in their performances. They were tight and tense. Sarah was free.

There is an analogy here in what Jesus is trying to communicate to Nicodemus and what Lent may offer us. There is, Jesus says, a freer world for us, a world where we can thrive and live fully, and we get at it by letting go of our egos in a particular way. Wouldn't it be great to be able to be like Sarah Hughes, to go out and have fun, to just be happy to be here, to act as if you have nothing to lose and everything to win!

That would nearly be it, except for one caveat. Jesus says to Nicodemus that the way to access the freer world, to be born from above, is to "act in truth." The Greek word is *aletheia*, to be transparent, to be open, to unveil oneself. Remember, Nicodemus has come to Jesus under cover of darkness; he wants to conceal himself and find out what Jesus has to say! And Jesus is saying, "Nicodemus, this is a pattern for you! The freedom you seek is in transparency – as transparent as wind and water – and in openness!"

What does the person who lives in the free world of transparency do differently than the one who lives in the world of constraint? For one thing, the transparent person does not bumble through life without self-examination. Without beating themselves up all the time, the free person can ask, "Do I value, appreciate, and strive for the open spaces of directness, or am I more covert, seeking protection in shadow and constraint?"

Simply asking the question is itself a freeing act, because it's already a gesture or act of openness or transparency. The answer, if we're honest, is always mixed. No one is completely transparent or covert. But all of us can ask the question of ourselves, of our trusted friends, and of our community. In so doing, we may see ourselves more clearly and experience the freedom of not having to be "right," but of being true.

That's what Jesus meant when he spoke of being "born from above." He wanted a truer world, a more transparent world where people would be freer to love and to be loved. In a moment of penetrating wisdom Frye wrote, "this other world is not up in the sky or waiting for us after death, but is directly in front of us...and we are living in it when we open our eyes and stop holding our breath."[12]

Nicodemus must have understood what Jesus was saying. He must have taken it to heart, because, as Frye observes, later we learn that it was Nicodemus – the one who first came to Jesus under cover of darkness – who took Jesus down from the cross.[13]

AN UNCOMMON STRANGER

I love the story of Jesus and the Samaritan woman (John 4:5–29). No matter how many times we read it, at every level it challenges us to think in new ways. That is true of most stories in the Bible, but especially of this one. Let's take it at its least complicated level and see what riches it provides.

Here we have Jesus at rest. He's tired, exhausted from his work. His disciples have gone to a nearby town to find food. He needs water. He *really* needs water. You don't go long in a desert or near-desert climate without water.

He encounters a person who has the wherewithal to give him the water he needs. She has the jug. However, this person is a Samaritan woman. In the culture of the time, it was unacceptable for males and females to interact or speak to each other in public. To complicate matters even more, Jews hated Samaritans, and the rabbis had particularly nasty things to say about Samaritan women.

Jesus is forced by his need for water to let all those boundaries fall, to let all of the false distinctions vanish, to let all of the laws erected to keep his people away from her people become petty and irrelevant. His pressing need forced him to encounter this person as a person first, and as a woman and a Samaritan second, or third, or not at all. It is such an important lesson to learn. When class, culture, and religion fall away, we are humans together.

I was horrified a few years ago by the bloodshed in India as Muslims and Hindus fought over the construction of a Hindu temple on the ruins of an ancient mosque. A train was attacked; a town was attacked in reprisal. The most horrible acts of murder were perpetrated against the innocent, day in and day out. This is what religious people, including Christians, do to each other from time to time, to our shame.

The encounter between Jesus and the Samaritan woman shows that if we encounter one another at what Frye called the level of primary concern, of our mutual need – for food and drink, for companionship and clothing and shelter, for freedom of movement – many of the beliefs that divide people melt away. The dispute between Muslims and Hindus in India may have been about many things – such as entitlement or cultural rights or who owns what – but it had little to do with religion. Religion at its best has to do with freedom and the language of love. Whenever religion is used to justify aggression, retribution, or hatred, it has been corrupted and co-opted by those with a non-religious agenda. Religious people sometimes forget that.

The story of the Samaritan woman also suggests that when we encounter one another on the basis of our common primary need, transformation is possible. So here we have Jesus with a basic human need, water, and a woman who can provide what he needs. The scene unfolds like a flower opening to the sunshine, though not a perfect flower, for it has some rough brown edges, as do all human interactions. The woman is concerned to point out to him what is expected of him from a cultural point of view. She chides him for being so needy that he forgets he shouldn't be asking a Samaritan woman for *anything*. She encounters him on a cultural and legal level. Jesus has his own cultural struggles – reminding her that salvation is from the Jews. But above all, he invites her to consider what is essential and what isn't. She will give him water; he will give her living water. She will give him water; he will give her freedom and the language of love. And that, it turns out, is exactly what *she* needs.

One Friday while I was studying theology, I was feeling drained from a particularly exhausting week. I sought a place for rest and I went to a lounge at the school to sit and read. Usually there was no one there; I could rely on that. On that Friday, however, as I climbed the stairs I was delighted to hear someone playing the grand piano, which sat in the middle of the room.

When I sat down on one of the couches, the person at the piano stopped playing. I got up to leave because I thought I was spoiling her concentration. Then she leaned over and said, "Excuse me. Would you mind making me nervous?"

I didn't hear her correctly. I replied, "Yes, I am," thinking she was asking if I was nervous, which I was.

She looked at me, puzzled. "I need someone to make me nervous, so I can play properly. I have a recital next week, and I need someone to make me nervous." She then offered to play her whole recital for me, if only I would sit and listen. I quickly agreed.

She played for an hour or so and I listened to every note, loving every minute of it. After the recital was over, to which I gave a round of applause, she came over, sat down, and asked me who I was. I told her I was a minister. She had never met one before. That's when I found out she was a Jew.

There was a subtle change at that point. Suddenly, the encounter took on our cultural baggage. She tensed up a bit. So did I. She decided to risk more, however, and asked why I needed Jesus. I was embarrassed by her directness. We talked theology for a while, but then the conversation drifted off and very soon we parted ways.

She had fed me with her music. I had fed her with my listening. In conversation, I was hesitant. She was hesitant. But even in hesitancy, when we encountered one another at the level of basic human need, we discovered a clearing where the sun shines and warms the soul. It was a warm moment that will stay forever in my memory. What happened? On one level not much. On another, everything.

In W. O. Mitchell's *Who Has Seen the Wind*, a little boy is growing up in a small town on the Saskatchewan prairie. His world is rich in experience and colour. At one point, he overhears a curious conversation between the village cobbler and the school principal. The cobbler says, "It's all inside of me...this shop's inside of me, this town's inside of me. Shoes, folks, churches, stores, grain elevators, farms, horses, dogs...all inside of me. You, the kids, this shop, inside of me...me inside of my shop; so that means I've got me inside of me. All I want know," he says, "is who the hell is me?"[14]

Who the hell is me? Christians answer this question with the person of Jesus, who reminds us how to be real with one another. Jesus reveals us to ourselves. That's why he's so important to us. Whenever Jesus encounters someone, he unveils them to themselves. He gives them freedom. He gives them the language of love. He gives them living water. He gives them the ability to rise above their secondary concerns and focus on their primary concerns, on their own humanity and the hu-

manity of others. His way of being with those he encounters shows us the way.

This is not merely academic. The instruction for us,
as we return to the story of Jesus and the Samaritan
woman, is how we might pursue more authentic human
relationships ourselves. When we approach a person on
the basis of essential human need – what unites, us not
what divides us – then there is a greater possibility that
our encounters with that person will have in them the
taste of freedom. It seems almost too simple, but there
it is. And it's a good thing to remember and to practice
on our Lenten journey.

YOU ARE WHO YOU ARE

One Good Friday after coffee with friends, I went into
a local coffee shop to buy beans. As I waited, I noticed
a member of my congregation having coffee with one of
her friends. Eventually, she came up to me as I waited
to be served at the counter. She didn't say hi, she just
started talking to me and we fell into conversation. We
had an easy affection for each other.

Her friend came up beside her, not knowing who I
was, and said to her, "Are you flirting with this man?"

She made some comment like, "Maybe!"

As I was leaving, I said to her behind my hand,
"Now you can tell her who I really am!"

Without missing a beat, she looked at me and said,
"You are who you really are!" And, of course, she was
right.

What a great way to talk about the moment just before we enter the empty tomb: "You are who you really are!"

Walter Brueggemann puts it this way: "[F]aith is the study of how God is more for us than we are for ourselves."[15] That's what Lent shows us. We find that God is on our side. None of those negative narratives our mind makes up about ourselves and that others make up about us really matter. What can separate us from this kind of love? Nothing. Nothing. Nothing.

Through Lent, we have followed a person named Jesus. Up until this final journey, we have learned that he is a teacher, a wise person, a spirit person, a prophet, a poet, a storyteller, a healer and now he is on a journey into serious trouble. He is put on trial for blasphemy. He is innocent (everyone knows it) and he is crucified anyway because, for the Romans, his life was less than worthless, and there were political issues to consider.

As it happens, Jesus wasn't only an innocent person. He was God's innocent person. At the crucifixion, we meet God's Friday, or what evolved to be called Good Friday. We witness the free giving by an innocent, and an overwhelming expression of love.

Frye says more.

A place of blood and terror is not the only place where God can be found, but it is the only kind of place where God can be born. For God can only be born in the context of God's wrath...the wrath of God is the revelation to [us] of the hell that [we have] made of [our] life on this earth...the death of Christ on the cross makes it possible for [us] to see a few other things besides hell.[16]

Among those "few other things" is the possibility of visionary acts and, to my mind, the most visionary acts are acts of forgiveness.

I am always moved by acts of forgiveness. They seem too rare these days. So many of the stories we read in books and watch in movies and hear about on the news operate on revenge. I was especially struck by a picture that appeared one Tuesday in Holy Week. It showed Cindy Wesley embracing a teenage girl who had been tried on a charge of uttering threats against Cindy's 14-year-old daughter, Dawn-Marie. Dawn-Marie had committed suicide after a group of girls, including the teenager in the picture, accused her of spreading gossip about them.

In a gesture of forgiveness, Cindy embraced one of her daughter's tormenters and said, "Do not hold yourself accountable for her death." The photograph of the embrace is achingly moving. The girl has her arms around Cindy's neck like a child. One of Cindy's hands gently touches the girl's hair and she looks at the girl with what can only be described as the deep compassion and tenderness of a loving mother.

For me, the photograph is about *all* parents and *all* children, and it represents God's Friday, Good Friday. Our aching numbness is met by God's own aching gesture of healing, and out of it comes the most supreme

LENT

love imaginable. We can only understand Good Friday
by this kind of analogy. God meets us with an embrace.
God aches for us. We ache for God. The meeting is
good, and the meeting is God's. That's why it's good.
That's why it's Good Friday.

Three days later there is another movement. If the
journey that ends in the arrest of Jesus is about God's
innocent one, and if Good Friday is about God and
about God's overwhelming love, then the resurrection
is all about *us*. The empty tomb is about *us*. The empty
tomb says, "You are who you really are." The empty
tomb is about something in this universe being more
for you than you are for yourself. The empty tomb is
about God being on your side.

Cindy's embrace of the girl who caused her daughter
so much pain, while being a story about unbelievable
forgiveness, is not a story about resurrection. Resurrection happens *after* the photograph, after the cameras are
gone and the media stops calling. Resurrection happens
when two lives are transformed by the deep compassion
of God. Resurrection happens when, on the third day,
one wakes up and things are different. Resurrection is
not about the empty tomb; it is about what we do after
we realize the tomb is empty.

Do you remember when Pope John Paul II was shot
by a disturbed Albanian man many years ago? The pope
suffered with the wound to his last breath. Remember
that the pope forgave him from his hospital room. But
that wasn't the end of it. He went to visit the man in

prison. The would-be assassin fell to his knees in the pope's presence and, later, John Paul campaigned for his early release.

It's about us. It's about how we respond to the good news. It's about what we do after we notice the empty tomb.

Many summers ago, in the Eastern Townships of Quebec, a car containing five young people plunged into a flooded quarry. Four were killed. The only survivor was the driver, Steve Rousseau, 21. At supper the following Monday, the parents of the dead young people gathered in a kitchen. Then they invited Mr. Rousseau and his parents to come over. The Rousseaus expected the worst. The tension in the room was high, but one by one the parents of the victims rose and told Mr. Rousseau that they forgave him.

None of us is quite Jesus. But we have probably seen and experienced this kind of visionary behaviour in our lives. We have seen and experienced these kind of echoes of the overwhelming love of God, and our lives are continually blessed by them. We are who we really are.

NOTES

1. Frye, *Collected Works*, 301.
2. Ibid., 367–368.
3. Dietrich Bonhoeffer, *Letters and Papers from Prison* (New York: Macmillan, 1971), 39.

4. Leonard Cohen, "Bird on the Wire," in *Stranger Music: Selected Poems and Songs* (Toronto: McClelland and Stewart, 1993), 144.

5. Dietrich Bonhoeffer, *Temptation*, trans. Kathleen Downham (London: SCM Press, 2013).

6. Frye, *Collected Works*, 368.

7. Ibid., 369.

8. Ibid.

9. Iris Murdoch, *The Sovereignty of the Good* (Oxford: Routledge, 2014), 82.

10. Reported in *The Guardian*, February 17, 2002. See https://www.theguardian.com/world/2002/feb/17/jamesastill.theobserver

11. Frye, Collected Works, 336.

12. Ibid.

13. Ibid., 335.

14. W. O. Mitchell, *Who Has Seen the Wind* (Toronto: McClelland and Stewart, 2001), 310.

15. Brueggemann, *Comes the Poet*, 36. He cross references Romans 8:31ff: "If God is in on our side, who is against us?"

16. Frye, *Collected Works*, 301.

EASTER

The god vanishes abruptly –
yet a great silence descends upon the earth
in which [the] presence is felt more strongly
than ever before.
  – Karen Armstrong, *The Spiral Staircase*[1]

When the disciples thought they had
lost Jesus ... they were found by him.
  – Karl Barth, *Church Dogmatics*[2]

That which is truly ourselves will never die.
  – Northrop Frye, *Collected Works*[3]

I N THE CHRISTIAN YEAR,
Easter is the fifth movement of a six-movement sym-
phony within the larger framework of the year as a
whole. We start with Advent and Christmas, preparing
for and then experiencing through the narrative of the
birth of Jesus, the birth or rebirth of spirit in our lives
through human community. This is followed by the
season of Epiphany, when we explore how unseen but

insistent and persistent spiritual truths are revealed to us and we are invited to open to them. During Lent, we follow Jesus on a road to certain death; we wonder at his ability to remain focused on his mission, and about those things that distract us from our own purpose. We experience the death itself on a day called Good Friday, or God's Friday. This journey of the innocent toward death invites us into a reflectiveness which offers a new freedom toward unexpected, counterintuitive, and healing behaviours. Finally, we find ourselves at resurrection, at Easter, a moment that expands into 40 days of celebration that show a change in the human situation, and perhaps in creation itself. These movements within the larger cycle of the Christian seasons reflect the movements in Jesus' life. They also reflect movements in our own lives, and in the life of the world.

DEEP COMPASSION MEETS THE ORDINARY

After the death of his wife, Joy Davidman, C. S. Lewis kept a journal chronicling his grieving progress. One night he wrote this.

A man in total darkness. He thinks he is in a cellar or dungeon. Then there comes a sound. He thinks it might be a sound from far off – waves or wind-blown trees or cattle half a mile away. And if so, it proves he's not [really] in a cellar, but free, in the open air. Or it's maybe a much smaller sound close at hand – a chuckle of laughter. And if

so, there is a friend just beside him in the dark ... Either
way [it is] a good, good sound.[4]

This is the sound of resurrection emanating from what
Northrop Frye and William Blake before him called
"the double vision."[5] The bleak facts present themselves
to us in the corporeal world and then, in company with
the biblical narrative, we engage in an "imaginative response," or what Søren Kierkegaard called a "leap," in
which the biblical narrative speaks to our own experience in the profoundest way. Experiences of resurrection find their way into the creative process as well,
which is why Frye was able to link the experience of
faith so closely to the function of literature and art.[6]

The day after her mother's funeral, the Canadian
poet Anne Carson sat down to "leaf through" the dia-
ries of Virginia Woolf. She found a part where Woolf
was reflecting on the death of her own father. Woolf
wrote that "forming such shocks into words and order
was the strongest pleasure known to me."[7] Carson had
already finished writing the book of poetry she was
working on. But at the end of that wonderful book she
included a little reflection on her mother and a picture
of them together when she was a child. She wrote, "For
death *although utterly unlike life* shares a skin with it."[8]
In darkness and in light, heart speaks to heart, ordering
grief into something beautiful. This, too, is double vision. This, too, is resurrection.

When ministers meet with bereaved families, it is a
sad gathering. The silences are deep and sonorous. Then,

without much warning, when the remembrances start coming, the sadness is punctuated by periods of laughter. There are waves of highs and lows, and the laughter washes over it all like a warm bath.

Such gatherings became the holiest time for me during my years as a minister, as families acted out what we know in our hearts to be true, as Frye observed: "That which is truly ourselves will never die," which to my mind is another way of saying, "the best in all of us will never die."[9] Once more, this is resurrection.

The psalmist put it like this: "goodness and kindness pursue me, every day of my life" (Psalm 23, JB).

In following the movements in Jesus' life before Good Friday, we observed that Jesus paid close attention to what God wanted him to do and be. He did not allow himself to be distracted from his mission. On that leg of the journey, during Lent, we were invited to ask ourselves how we too might pay close attention and not be distracted in our own lives.

A traditional response to that question suggests that we should give up "self." But the greater problem in our time is that we often don't give ourselves *enough* time and space. As the sublime Gregory Baum put it, "It is not that we love ourselves too much but that we do not love ourselves at all."[10]

Unlike Jesus, most of us are not on the road to our own imminent, violent death and do not have to pay close attention to our life's purpose at the same time. Although the imminence of death may concentrate the mind, that is typically *not* the immediate challenge we face. Rather, the challenge for most of us is that we become distracted from our life's mission, what the ancient English called our *wyrd*, by distractions in our lives. Trouble at work. The death of a loved one. Illness. Accident. The promise of resurrection, the promise of Easter, is that if we can continue to care for ourselves even in crisis; if we can succeed, even marginally, in paying close attention to what is wanted of us, even during our own Good Fridays, we may experience a breakthrough of sorts – an appearance, a vision, a fine final movement.

Two of Jesus' disciples discovered this truth on the Emmaus road, a story told in Luke's gospel (Luke 24:1–12). As they walk towards the village of Emmaus, the two disciples talk about the crucifixion of Jesus, which has just happened. Suddenly, a stranger appears beside them and accompanies them through the next number of hours explaining the scriptures and Jesus' words to them. Then, when everything is as clear as it can be, their companion disappears.

Maybe it was Jesus, risen. But the question of the identity of the stranger may be less important than the process the disciples were caught up in.

Early that same day at Jesus' tomb, Mary Magdalene, a disciple of Jesus, thought she saw a gardener near the tomb, and then she was sure it was Jesus. Why not?

In yet another story, the disciples struggle to catch fish all night in the Sea of Tiberias, or Sea of Galilee. Then, at the break of dawn, they see a figure preparing breakfast on the shore.

Appearances. At the tomb. On the road. On the shoreline.

Augustine said it this way in his *Confessions*: "You were there in front of me, but I had wandered away from myself. And if I could not find my own self, how much less could I find You?"[11]

If we can stick it out. If we can stay with the dark night of the soul. If we can put in the time on our Good Fridays and care for ourselves all the while, Easter promises that a breakthrough will come in time.

This is how Frye thought of resurrection. It was not a mere revival of a dead body, but a depiction of how God can bring time to a kind of standstill; when, in the living of our lives, we may appropriate our past and our future in an instant, in one moment, a focused beam of light.

The writer of the Gospel of John calls it eternal life, a much misunderstood phrase. What he means is that for disciples of Jesus, and we might say for other people too, it is possible to live life in God's life, in what theologians like to call "the eternal now." Karen Armstrong calls it the "strong presence."[12] It is hard to find the language for it. But by living in this way, in this time, we come to understand how we must live to help make our time more fruitful for ourselves, for the human community, for the earth, and for its creatures.

If anyone needs this message, I certainly do. When I am under stress or facing some challenge or struggle, I want it to be over yesterday. I want and need closure. And yet, I know that I am somehow better for those times when closure is *not* given so fast, when only the slow progress of time can be counted on, when desolation more than consolation dominates. That is, when resolution or closure finally *does* come, a little resurrection happens and I am larger in myself than I was before. Life is richer, dearer, and more precious.

GOING ON AHEAD, A LITTLE

A little girl visited the local corner store just before Easter. The store was replete with every kind of Easter treat, including chocolate bunnies, just sitting out in the open. The little girl loved chocolate more than anything in the world but she knew that she couldn't, or shouldn't, have any Easter chocolate before Easter morning. She stood looking at the row of chocolate bunnies. She looked at them from one side. She looked at them from the other side.

Then, without quite knowing what she was doing or why, while her mother was busy with the shopkeeper and no one was looking, the little girl picked up one of the chocolate bunnies, turned it over, picked off the tiny spherical tail, and popped it into her mouth. Then she put the bunny back where it had been.

The little girl savoured the texture and the taste of the chocolate as it melted slowly in her mouth. And then it was gone.

She looked at the row of bunnies again. Her hands became clammy and a wave of hot embarrassment passed over her. She was horrified. Far from being unnoticeable, the missing tail looked like a giant gash on the back of the chocolate bunny. Someone was bound to notice and she would be blamed. She knew what she had to do.

A few minutes later, her mother reappeared and beckoned. The little girl was strangely quiet, but she put her hand in her mother's hand and they walked out together into the spring sunshine.

Later that day, the shopkeeper called to his wife.

"Gladys, look at this! It's the strangest thing."

"What is it?" she asked.

"Look at all these chocolate bunnies," he said. "All their tails are missing!"[13]

It strikes me that, in our time as a society, we have done much the same thing to Jesus. So many people have tried to solve the "problem" of Jesus by chipping away at him, so to speak. Think of Dan Brown and the great success of his novel *The DaVinci Code*, or Nicos Kazantzakis' *The Last Temptation of Christ*, or José Saramago's *The Gospel According to Jesus Christ*. There's also Ann Rice's *Christ the Lord*, and Colm Toiban's *The Testament of Mary*. Amazon lists more than 3,000 books about Jesus. Some of these books have been turned into Hollywood blockbusters, joining other films made by everyone from Cecil B. DeMille, to Mel Gibson, to James Cameron.

For the last century, New Testament scholars have been trying by various hermeneutic means to uncover the historical Jesus. Which of the words attributed to him in the various gospels did he really utter? There has been more scholarly literature written about Jesus in the last 50 years than all scholarly literature in the previous 1,900 years.

We are a culture obsessed with Jesus. Why? What is it we want from this person?

Maybe it's just human nature. Maybe we want to see if, by illuminating what is hidden from us by history or text, by depicting him again and again in print, in film, or in whatever medium we have at hand, we can, by our efforts, discover the truth once and for all. We want to settle the matter like a Sudoko puzzle. We want a hook to hang the mystery on.

But maybe we should ask ourselves what we would do differently if we actually found Jesus?

Watching the James Cameron documentary in which the sarcophagus of Jesus is purportedly uncovered, I asked myself how my faith would be different if we could prove that the bones of Jesus were buried with the bones of Mary Magdalene, and I realized my faith wouldn't be different at all.

So what *does* my faith rely on? The power of the story of Jesus. The power of the teachings of Jesus. The power of the people, ordinary folk like you and me, who found a power or love in themselves, or for one another and for the world, that they could not have imagined before. People such as Peter, James, Mary, Paul, Augustine, Luther, Wesley, Simone Weil, Martin Luther King, Jr., and so many more. My faith relies on the power of the people in our own community, the great power they have that we sometimes miss in our determination to uncover Jesus somewhere else. What if we already had more than enough in the narrative, right here and now, to realize that our lives have already changed, as has the life of the world?

Anyone who has read a book about Jesus, or gone to a movie about Jesus, or ventured to the holy land or to France to discover him, are like those first disciples at the tomb that first Sunday morning looking for a body! We want substance. We want something material to gaze upon. Some "body" to touch. But to quote Mark's gospel, the reality is, "He is not here!... He's going on ahead of you!" (Mark 16:5–7).

"He's going ahead of you!" Now there's a thought. He's going ahead of you. He is *always* ahead of us. Just ahead. Just a little beyond our reach. And no matter how we search the facts, the record, the story, the manuscripts, the ossuaries, he will always be just a little ahead. How frustrating! How maddening!

But what if that were enough? What if it were enough to know that he's going on ahead of us? What if we ceased to be concerned about the deficits in our knowledge – the facts, the details, the science – and just relied on what we already have? Rather than concern ourselves with what is missing – like the shopkeeper with the chocolate bunnies – what if we focused on what we have at hand?

Could it be enough to stop looking ahead at what we don't have, turn around in our tracks, and try to discern instead what we have yet to see, what has already happened but has escaped our notice or understanding?

It reminds me of the story of four travellers who were at a conference in the Philippines. They stayed talking too long and arrived very late at the local airport. Grabbing their bags from the taxi they ran into the terminal. One of them, in his haste, knocked over a table on which a local girl had some items for sale. Being late and not wanting to miss their flight, they ran on, cleared security, and arrived at the gate just before it closed.

As they hastened across the tarmac towards their waiting plane, one of them stopped, said farewell to his amazed colleagues, and returned to the terminal. When he got back to the table, he discovered that the girl was nine years old and blind. Some of the jars she had been selling were broken. He helped her clean up the mess as best he could and then said to her, "Here's 50 dollars to cover the cost of whatever is broken." As he walked away, she called after him, "Sir, are you Jesus?"

The traveller might well have replied, "No, he is not here. He's gone ahead of us a little."

HEAD AND HEART

The trouble is that the question about Jesus' "body" – which is what so much of our interest boils down to – is a head question. But if I believe, I believe with my heart.

Trying to answer the head question – the absent body question – forces me to become defensive somehow. After all, bodies don't just disappear. And the logicians in the crowd want to stop you in your tracks, put their hands on your shoulders, look you in the eye and say, "Do you believe it actually happened or not?"

Marilynne Robinson put it well when she said, "Nothing true can be said about God from a posture of defense."[14] It's best not to get trapped like that. It's a case of apples and oranges. The question about the missing body is asking about stones. But we're talking about visions here. That's the difference. Stones and visions don't exist in the same faith universe.

From a heart perspective, the day of Jusus' resurrection became more remarkable over time for the disciples. It's often the same way with us. You know that kind of day. As Marilynne Robinson describes in her novel *Gilead*, "[T]he visionary aspect of [it] comes to you [as you remember it] or it opens to you over time..." You discover a truth about the day as more days pass. Like the day you fell in love for the first time. Or like the day your friend told you the truth about yourself and you turned on her and vowed never to speak her again – and still you mourn that break, even as you continue to love and seek love and find love.

In the novel *The Master*, Colm Toibin tries to capture the process of grief as Henry James mourns the suicide of the woman closest to him in his adult life. "[T]he pain of living without her," he writes, "was no more than a penalty he paid for the privilege of having been young with her."

Or maybe the day of the resurrection was like the day after the ice storm, when Frye pulled open the curtains and saw in a bush a blue jay on one side and a cardinal on the other.

The memory of these kinds of days is enough to make one weep.

That is how it was for the disciples. Things became clearer as they remembered the day. They dreamed *forward* as they remembered the day when Jesus *wasn't* there and yet *was*. The deep mystery of this occasion is that it became a power that helped them live into the future. That is the *unique* part of resurrection. The stone was rolled away and in the uncovered hollow they found a dream that became bread for the journey.

And that is the amazing thing for us, too. There are so many stories from life that remind us of resurrection day. Easter is a story event that reaches out for more personal stories of healing and restoration. Stories about real people – like the daughter who interrupted her young life after university, forsaking a promising career and even the promise of marriage, to return home and care for her dying mother. The relationship between this mother and daughter had always been marked by tension and angry standoffs. In the last few years they could hardly bear to be in the same room with each other. It was as if they were fighting all the time for some imaginary piece of ground between them. And yet the daughter went home to tend to her dying mother. She was dreaming forward. She had a vision of resurrection. And on the day she died, her mother said what she had never said before: "I love you." The stone was rolled away for the daughter and in the uncovered hollow she found a dream that became strength for her journey. That is what resurrection is.

As we live into the resurrection story, things become possible that seemed impossible before. Possibility opens to us like a flower opens in springtime. All stones are rolled away and dreaming into the future becomes not only possible, but practical too.

It's a heart thing.

HOW WAS JESUS DIFFERENT?

I wept after hearing of the death of Pope John Paul II. This surprised me, because I disagreed with so much of what he taught, from doctrine to social issues. Yet I was *not* surprised when they made him a saint, even though the practice is somewhat foreign to me.

I remember his first trip to Canada in the 1980s. I observed him closely, recording his visit which was broadcast live on the CBC. I was in my second parish. I noted how he touched the sick and called them beautiful. I wept then, too. I noted how he took the children and kissed them and let them kiss him back. How he covered their small heads with his hands. How he moved forward to greet people with both his hands extended. Later, I followed his pastoral activities very closely: how he visited his would-be assassin in prison and lobbied for the man's early release. And then, in his final years,

I observed his great courage while his body let him down. Surely there was more than a little of God's intentional love in this pope, pastor to the disinherited of the world.

No doubt his teaching, even his great learnedness will fade with time, especially considering the strides taken by Pope Francis. What will last is the memory of those moments of touching, for these gestures outlast all ideas and all truths. Indeed, of all things human, acts of love are the greatest, most eternal. They last forever.

We know this because of the witness of a person named Jesus, whose deep compassion for the world could not be contained by the grave, whose deep compassion now permeates the world he wept to leave, coaxing every hope beyond itself.[15] But how did this come to be? How was this Jesus any different than the rest of us?

Do you remember how the great comic actor W. C. Fields became a star in show business? When he first started out in vaudeville, he made it as a performer because he had a natural genius for juggling. In fact he was so good that audiences seemed to resent the perfection of his juggling. When, during one performance he accidentally dropped something and recovered with a sardonic and self-deprecating ad lib, he got a laugh. Soon he was deliberately putting mistakes (and drawling his comments on them) into his act. A star was born.[16]

That so often happens, doesn't it? We bumble into what we are meant to do and be. We work hard in one area of endeavour and find our place somewhere else by accidental opportunity. Very few of us actually move through our life with such intentionality that we know from the beginning exactly what we are doing, why we are doing it, and where we are going to end up. That's mostly because we are truly creatures of our human world; we are not only born into it, but it shapes us and molds us.

True genius, on the other hand, has its own kind of destiny. When we think of Mozart and all the music he composed in his short life, when we consider the sheer force of his creative power, the way the beauty of his work wills or draws our attention, it's almost as if the other people in his life were accidents to his sublime accomplishment.

Virginia Woolf, too, in some sense, shone larger than all others in her circle with her own creative genius. She had access to her father's amazing library as she was growing up. Conversation with her siblings and closest friends sparkled like no other. Leonard Woolf, her husband, painstakingly distracted her from her demons all those years as long as he possibly could. It was as if she existed in her own protected realm and others were forced to adapt.

Vincent van Gogh, once he left lay preaching and found his paints and his way of painting, was consumed by a kind of madness in his need to create in his own way. No one except his brother Theo seemed to have any idea of the urgency of his calling. In the end, he was not a painter with paints so much as he was the brush and the paint itself, willing their way compulsively onto any canvas that would present itself.

When we think of Jesus of Nazareth we are forced to consider a unique case. Unlike our own bumbling adaptive ways, unlike even the geniuses we witness from time to time – whose qualities of achievement find their way by sheer brilliance, force of will, or oddity into the arena of historical recognition – Jesus' life was different. There was genius to be sure, but here is the real difference: his was a life of true, unwavering, pinpoint-accurate intentionality.

Once, when Frye presided at the funeral of a friend, all his ideas about the presence of the eternal in ordinary life came to the fore. He said, "That which is truly ourselves will never die."[17] When we think about our own "true self" over the span of our lives, we are likely to realize that this "true self" has only shone intermittently. When it comes to Jesus, I like to think his "true self" shone his whole life.

The mystery of the person Jesus is that even though the gospel accounts differ we know it is the same person. When he meets his end in a farcical trial and a horrible crucifixion, and when we witness, with those first disciples, that empty tomb and those appearances, we see continuity; we witness a special kind of intentionality that has a unity from the beginning of his ministry through to his death, and to his reputed life after death. In his life, people are not accidents that allow genius to shine forth. Rather, everyone he encounters is invited to see how love functions in this world, and how powerful love is even in the face of the sheer terror of a police state.

The Bible marks Jesus not as it does Elijah and Moses, as a person who is rewarded for his obedience; the Bible marks Jesus as the one, the only person, who was able in his life, his death, and his apparent life after death, to love the world throughout.

Emily Dickinson, in a rare affirmation of the miraculous in religion, says that there was something about Jesus as a person that a tomb could not contain.[18] This is a poet's way of seeing something important from a unique perspective. I find something profoundly true in this, from a faith standpoint. So intentional was Jesus in life for love that death, the ordinary human obstacle, was a boundary that could not contain him.

Interestingly, Marilynne Robinson says that it was the combination of this largeness of heart and the fact he was so sharply missed and so powerfully remembered that the disciples' desperate need drew him forth to them after death.[19] I like that idea too.

Every faithful person has their reasons for finding Jesus unique. For some, the miracles tug at the heart; for others the teaching; for others the personal experience. For me it has, from an early date, been the parables that touched me to my core. His keen knowledge of the presence of the "Other" in the world, and of how it operates in the world, and of the pressing need to pay attention, converts me over and over again from being a skeptic to a believer, in my own way.

My heart is what tells the story. How could he know that and not be unique, I ask myself. I do not say this to many people because it seems facile, as if I need to prove Jesus' singularity when my heart is what convinces me. But if we see his intentionality and its completeness from beginning to end, perhaps resurrection can begin to make some sense for us. What I mean is not *his* resurrection so much as resurrection itself. In my own view, Jesus opened the concept as an everyday experience.

Beyond the bumbling adaptiveness of the ordinary, or even the sheer creative force of genius, faithful people believe that resurrection is, in Marilynne Robinson's words, "a vast energy of intentional love that continues to surround us."[20] Love, as verb, communicates with us as never before, urging us to embrace it, coaxing every hope beyond itself in the person of Jesus.

EMMAUS

I love the story of the road to Emmaus. It's like a mystery novel. The whole scene feels shrouded and misty. It is the strange story of two disciples walking down a road to a town that archeologists have never found. We never hear about this fellow Cleopas again. The other disciple with him isn't even named, although tradition has it that it was Luke himself, or perhaps a female member of that early community.

These are not the big guns, the big names, the future stars of the Christian church. These two are ordinary people. Common folk. Not the great orators, nor the masters of argument, nor the brilliant theologians who can tell you how many angels dance on the head of a pin. Here we are bothered in an extraordinary way by ordinary people. Hallelujah! That's why I love this story.[21]

And what are these little people of the early church experiencing that anyone should bother with them? They are involved in a great tragedy. They are in the midst of a profound brokenness. They are leaving Jerusalem, which has become a city of death. And it is not an inconsiderable death. The death of Jesus represents the death of all their dreams, the death of all they hoped for. Killed by the authorities.

And there they are. Hit by a two-by-four called disappointment. Dazed. Walking, seemingly aimlessly, because there seems to be no place to go, nothing else to do.

What this story says to me is that regardless if I am on the right road, whatever that might be, or even on the road to nowhere, even if I am confused and a little dazed, there is a companion that comes and walks with me. In other words, *we* may be dazed and confused, but the companion is never confused about us.

Ernest Shackleton made a disastrous expedition to the South Pole. It was a magnificent failure. He went to cross the continent of Antarctica, but his ship Endurance got stuck in the ice and he spent a year traversing ice flows, paddling in rowboats, sailing a makeshift craft, and climbing over a mountain with one goal – to save every member of his expedition from freezing and starvation.

After arriving in Buenos Aires after the ordeal, he wrote to his wife: "I have done it...not a life lost and we have been through hell."[22] No mention of the failure – only the success, coming out the other side.

Shackleton wrote in his memoir *South* that as he and two others made a 36-hour march across South Georgia Island to a whaling station in hope of rescue, "it seemed to me often that we were four, not three."

A nurse in a critical care unit of a hospital told me once that when she and a doctor were working on a trauma patient – she on one side of the bed, the doctor on the other – she always had the impression there was a fourth person at the end of the bed.

"When I am playing a concert," says Anton Kuerti, the great Canadian pianist, "I...suspend my disbelief. I'm not into mysticism, but I try to persuade myself that if I play well enough, the incarnation of Beethoven will appear somewhere in the corner of the stage. It helps to make the performance special to me..."[23]

The disciples may have been on the road to Emmaus, but they probably felt as if they were headed nowhere; their hopes had been dashed; their lives on the brink – a resurrection formula. For it is in times such as this that our hearts may feel strangely warmed, when transformation may happen. That is when an empty tomb may yield meaning. That is when a kind of faith may be kindled.

T. S. Eliot picked up Shackleton's story and built the last section of his great 20th-century poem *The Waste Land* around it.

Who is the third who walks always beside you?
When I count, there are only you and I together ·
But when I look ahead up the white road
There is always another one walking beside you
Gliding wrapt in a brown mantle, hooded
I do not know whether a man or a woman
– But who is that on the other side of you?[24]

Despite the fact that we live in a global village, a world made small through communications technology and travel, we still feel lonely and isolated from one another, perhaps more so now than ever before. Yet the Emmaus road story, Shackleton's experience, this powerful poem, and the experiences of ordinary people can provide an antidote for the ills of our age. Emmaus suggests that a spirit *in* us, a spirit *beside* us, a spirit *with* us may yet bring the human family together in an absolute way.

We may not know where we will find the consolation or the presence we need, or how or when we will find it. But the universal spirit is among ordinary people like us who are open to the possibility that despite all appearances to the contrary, we will not be abandoned.

ORDINARY AND STRANGE

I love the story of Emmaus because, in it, Jesus is ordinary too. At Emmaus, the two disciples finally recognize Jesus when he breaks the bread. After he disappears, the two companions start back to Jerusalem in high spirits, radically changed, to tell their friends. They turned around and went back to the city of their buried hopes because he who had kindled that hope in the first place was with them. He who had brought that bread into their lives was with them after all. It was truly a miracle, a revelation, a moment with the eternal in it.

Up to that point, Jesus was concealed from the two disciples in this story by his ordinariness.[25] I think this is key to a universal understanding of Easter. Easter may be revealed to us in the ordinary world that you and I live in. We don't have to look for signs and wonders; they walk beside us every single day, in the ordinary people we encounter in our lives.

I had the honour of officiating at the memorial service of a beloved woman. She was ordinary, but her story wasn't. At the service, one of her office colleagues said this quite remarkable thing to her husband; he said that when he and the rest of his colleagues went home at night after being with her during the day, they wanted to be better people for their families. This woman didn't know it, but she was the risen one to her office colleagues.

She was ordinary. *They* were ordinary. And something that she said and did during their life together inspired a kind of intentionality in their lives – which is precisely what the resurrection is, what Easter is, and what the empty tomb means. Events of a resurrection kind in the ordinary world are often understood only as we look back over the encounter.

I also love the story of Emmaus because attention is given to the stranger. In times of anxiety and uncertainty, the stranger often becomes the scapegoat: the Jew in Nazi Germany, the Ba'hai in Iran, the Muslims in Bosnia, the Palestinians in Israel, the Kurds in Turkey, the Rohingya in Myanmar. But in the community of which Jesus is a part, we are called into another kind of story. These people on the road to Emmaus, even in their confusion and distress, seem to have some confidence that the truth will be revealed to them. Their open and searching curiosity is all that holds them up and, as it turns out, it is a stranger who reveals the truth they are looking for.

The Emmaus road story tells us that the stranger is not to be feared. The stranger is to be welcomed, for he or she may be Jesus in a stranger's clothing.

At one time, all of us were strangers, and then someone made us feel at home. Whoever reached out their hand to us and helped us over that threshold, whoever that stranger was, became Jesus for us for a time.

When I think about it, I have learned a lot from strangers. Once, I took a brief golf holiday in Virginia. One day I found myself golfing with some Vietnam veterans who worked out of Washington, D.C. They were great golfers. I was a hack. But they were very patient with me. At one point, the fellow I was riding in the cart with said to me, "You struggle well, Don." He was talking about my golf game, of course. But his words always come back to me when I am struggling and they could be my epitaph: "He struggled well." Perhaps that stranger was Jesus for me that day when he told me a truth about myself that I could always cherish.

The risen Christ, this mystery person, is hard to pin down. Is he over there or over here? Is she on the right or on the left? Is he in Abraham Lincoln or in Nelson Mandela? Is she in the innocence of our children or in the wisdom of St. Augustine? Is she in the gentle hands of Mother Teresa or in the prison warden at the jail? Is she in our insistent mother or in our distant father, in our friend who knows us well or in our boss who knows our work habits? Is he in the silence of the mountain meadow or in the raucous sunset on the lake? Is she in the words of the poem or in the music of Mozart? Is he in the darkness of the starry night or in the light of a dawning day? The road to Emmaus teaches us that the best news about ourselves may be in all those places, in all those people. And in the open space in *us*. But we need another kind of seeing, another kind of hearing to find it.

The person in the Emmaus story is no ghost, that's certain. This person is using all that makes us human to get across his message. Not only does he use language, he enters into the lives of the two disciples. He travels with them; he agrees to be their companion. And finally, he enters the most intimate signal of community; he breaks bread with them. The road to Emmaus may be a Bible story, but its message is universally true for all.

The risen Christ is among the common people, in the midst of tragedy and brokenness and confusion, among those who are open to believing they will not be abandoned. She is the stranger. We are uncertain of where or when or who she is. He comes in mystery. He asks us to see in a new way, to count him in. She comes to us in *her* humanity to all the aspects and complexities of *our* humanity.

In the story, the stranger might have gone further to another town, to other people, but at the bidding of the two disciples, he stayed with them in their grief and in their confusion, and so he stays with us as we constantly call upon him to be with us. Don't leave! Please stay with us.

On a trip to Washington, D.C., a few years ago, I was rechristened; "Sugar" became my new name. It was my first morning in Washington and I had just eaten a breakfast that was far too expensive. The waitress had been kind. I knew that the cost was not her fault and I tipped her generously as I always do. (I have a great appreciation for waiters and waitresses, since I was a failure as a waiter myself.) She seemed to be surprised by the tip. And then, as I left, she said, "See ya, sugar." It made my day! I chuckled about it all day long and wrote about it to one of my children that evening. Just thinking about it comforted my anxiety as I was getting acclimatized to an unfamiliar city.

At 5:30 one morning in May, Catherine Gildiner headed to the local park just off Bloor Street in Toronto, Ontario. (This was early in her life, before she became a clinical psychologist and bestselling author.) She had her infant twins with her, and her two-year-old son. The twins had been crying – they were inconsolable – and the trip to the park was a desperate effort to find some respite. When Catherine arrived at the park, no one was there except for one woman reading a book. The woman was in her 50s or 60s. The twins were screaming, both wanting to be fed, but Catherine could feed only one at a time. The woman didn't say anything; she never asked if Catherine needed help. She just took one of the babies and walked around with him until he stopped crying. Catherine fed the other. The stranger also engaged the two-year-old with his collection of hockey cards.

Catherine said later, "We sat there together on the park bench. We watched the sun come up and all the children were content. They heard the first birds of spring and saw the dew on the still-closed daffodils as they shone as yellow fists in the new sunlight."

About a year later, Catherine was walking down Bloor Street with her husband. The twins were in a double stroller; the older boy perched on his father's shoulders. Catherine caught sight of the stranger who had helped her that day, and pointed her out to her husband. Her husband said, "That's Jane Jacobs. She is probably the most famous city planner that ever lived!" [26]

One fall day just before worship I had a visit from a man who didn't know his own name. That Sunday we had announced worship with bagpipes – an instrument designed to deliver a musical message for miles around. And it did. The man who didn't know his own name heard it. In a state of fearful confusion, somehow he knew within himself that a church would be a safe place. I was busy getting ready for worship, but his plaintive tone told me that I had better pay attention. A man with no name, a stranger, had come in out of the cold to me.

For a short while after his visit, there was a media frenzy and I was in the middle of it. Then the story of the stranger who didn't know his own name became yesterday's news. Just like that. That's when I began to realize the spiritual significance of the Emmaus story. The corporate aspect of my job necessitated that I focus on the needs of the group rather than the needs of the individual. And yet right before me that Sunday was an individual need that took precedence over nearly everything else I had to do that morning. My "normal" did not count for as much as I thought. The extraordinary, intruding as it does, was telling me something I needed to know about my own mission in the world, just as it had for the disciples after Easter morning, for the couple on the road to Emmaus, for me in Washington, for Catherine Gildiner.

The "stranger," the risen Christ, may meet us anywhere, any time, in any person, and through those resurrection appearances we may find resurrection in our own lives. I take the story of the disciples on the road to Emmaus to mean, among a host of other things, that I am not in control of the resurrection. Its movement towards me is far more important than my movement towards it. The Emmaus road story teaches me the less audacious alternative. Watch and listen very carefully to the witness of the freedom of the world. Be curious. Be open to the stranger and to the strange.

ASCENSION: SHARDS OF LIGHT

There is popular story to the effect that when the Soviet Union put the first man in space in 1961, cosmonaut Yuri Gagarin said that he looked around but could not see God. There is good evidence from the available transcripts that he never said this, but even if he *had* said it he would have been speaking ironically. He knew very well that no one really believed he would see God. At the time, however, many of us in the West still spoke of a God "up there," or Jesus "up there" – many still do – even though we had long stopped believing that God resides on a cloud somewhere.

If we no longer take such vertical references literally, how might we look at the story of the ascension of Jesus (Luke 24:50–53)? In his book *The Double Vision*, Frye illustrated how the "up" part forms an essential part of the Christian metaphor of the cross. At his birth, Jesus comes "down" to the horizontal plane, the earth, the arena of human community. After the crucifixion he descends to the nether regions of death. At the resurrection, he rises again to the earth. And then at the ascension he "rises" again, effectively to the place from which he began. As a whole, this movement takes the form of a cross. It's helpful to note that the up-and-down vertical movement is also intended as a metaphor for how God transcends our usual notions of time, which we typically think of, or portray, as a horizontal line.[27]

Still, many of us today struggle with vertical images, as our metaphorical language has shifted towards images of God's immanence. The writer of Luke's gospel tells us that 40 days after Jesus rose from the dead and after many appearances to his disciples, Jesus "was lifted up while they all looked on, and taken from their sight." As a preacher, I was in the habit of assuming, along with Frye, that the biblical story was told to teach something that is important to know.[28] So let's put brackets around "the lifted up" part and see where we get.

At its simplest, the story of the ascension signifies that 40 days following Easter, Jesus returned to the place from which he had come having made a difference not only to human affairs but to the creation itself.

If you think this is a fantastic notion, consider mothers. Anna Quindlen, the American author, whose mother had been dead for 25 years, wrote somewhere, "I've needed my mother many, many times over the last 25 years, but she has never been there, except in my mind, where she tells me to buy quality, keep my hair off my face, and give my father the benefit of the doubt." There is a deep, lingering quality to a mother's love.

Rose Kennedy, the mother of a president and two senators put it this way: "Whenever I held my newborn baby in my arms, I used to think that what I said and did to [them] could have an influence not only on [them] but on all whom [they] met, not only for a day or a month but for all eternity..."[29]

Many mothers speak of a deep and abiding quality to motherhood, of a "first day for the rest of time" quality the day their child is born, of a sense that what they do may have an impact not only on their own child, but on generations to come.

In a larger sense, that is what the ascension of Jesus means – that the profundity of his life and of his death and of his life after death continues to affect the entire human community and the creation besides. The ascension signifies that though the world may be broken and bent in some pretty fundamental ways, shards of light have been dispersed to the darkest corner.

In Leonard Cohen's song "Anthem," he reminds us that everything has a crack in it: "that's how the light gets in."

That's another way to see the ascension. Even though we may have suffered tremendous pain and heartbreak, we can cast a glance back and look at the cracks where the light got in, and give thanks for that which no darkness can ever master.

So ascension may not signify so much a "lifting up" as a "lifting out," a dispersal of shards of light into all corners of creation. Jesus appeared among his disciples for 40 days after Easter to help them grasp the reality of another kind of presence in the world. Then, according to the story, he was taken from their sight. His light was dispersed into the creation that bore him. Jesus had come out of a spiritually rich human community. He was produced by real people – he had a mother and a father, and he had a special relationship with God. More than that, he was a product of this earth, as we are. At the ascension, he returned to that earth, to the common life of all people, and into the arms of his God – all at the same time.

Christians who say that Christ is not present in any but the Christian community, or in any but their own particular Christian community, haven't taken the ascension seriously. The story of the ascension represents no less than the radical notion that God's spirit may be found in all places and creatures, not just in *our* places and in *our* community. The implications of this are enormous. It means that holiness resides not only among the faithful who gather in our own communities, but resides everywhere.

Shards of light travelling out.

NOTES

1. Armstrong, *Spiral Staircase*, 302.
2. Karl Barth, *Church Dogmatics*, eds. G. W. Bromley and T. F. Torrence, vols. 1–2 (New York: T&T Clark,1960), 114.
3. Frye, *Collected Works*, 291.
4. C. S. Lewis, *A Grief Observed* (San Francisco: HarperSanFrancisco, 1994), 63–64, 81.
5. Frye, *Double Vision*, 22–28.
6. Frye, *Collected Works*, 8.
7. As quoted in Anne Carson, *Men in the Off Hours* (New York: Alfred A. Knopf, 2000), 165. See also her poignant reflection on a visit to her mother as she contemplates the life of Emily Brontë and the end of a love affair in *Glass, Irony & God* (New York: New Directions Books, 1995), 138.

8. Ibid., 166.
9. Frye, *Collected Works*, 291.
10. Gregory Baum, *Man Becoming: God in Secular Experience* (New York, The Seabury Press, 1970).
11. St. Augustine, *Confessions*, V.ii.2 http://spot.colorado.edu/~pasnau/inprint/plot.htm
12. Armstrong, *Spiral Staircase*, 302.
13. Julie Beaudoin gave me the bones of this story in *The Globe and Mail*, Friday, April 6, 2007, A12.
14. Marilynne Robinson, *Gilead* (Toronto: Harper Collins, 2004), 177.
15. The phrase "wept to leave" is from Marilynne Robinson's very helpful discussion of the resurrection in *The Death of Adam: Essays on Modern Thought* (New York: Mariner Books, 1998), 239.
16. R. Schicken in a review of *W.C. Fields: A Biography* by J. Curtis, in *New York Times Book Review*, March 30, 2003.
17. Frye, *Collected Works*, 291.
18. Emily Dickenson, "Obtaining but our own Extent," poem #1543, the text of which is "Obtaining but our own Extent / in whatsoever Realm– / 'Twas Christ's own personal Expanse / That bore him from the Tomb–"
19. Robinson, *Death of Adam*, 234.
20. Ibid.
21. My thanks to the Rev. Dr. Victor Shepherd for this great insight.
22. Letter to his wife Emily, Sept 3, 1916, https://www.spri.cam.ac.uk/archives/shackleton/articles/1537,2,32,15.html.

23. Artist's Life, *Globe and Mail*, April 28, 2001, https:// www.theglobeandmail.com/arts/anton-kuerti/article4146954/

24. Eliot, *Complete Poems and Plays*, 48.

25. Robinson, *Adam*, 242.

26. I lifted this story from an article that appeared in *The Globe and Mail,* January 11, 2015. I no longer know the author's name nor the title of the piece.

27. Frye, *Double Vision*, 46.

28. Ibid., 76–77.

29. My thanks to Michael Kesterton for these quotes. Facts and Arguments, *The Globe and Mail*, Friday, May 1, 2002.

PENTECOST

Whatever is struck by fire from the sky…is symbolically at
the highest point in the world.
— Northrop Frye, *The Great Code*[1]

[L]anguage is just about the only thing that fights for
genuine humanity in this blinded world.
— Northrop Frye, *Collected Works*[2]

PENTECOST IS THE LONGEST
SEASON IN THE CHURCH CALENDAR. It begins 40 days after
Easter Sunday, on Pentecost Sunday, and extends all the
way to the first Sunday of Advent, closing the circle of the
year. The *day* of Pentecost itself did not start out as a
Christian holy day at all. Prior to its appropriation or transformation by Christianity, Pentecost, or *Shavuot*, was one
of three major Jewish holy days. If a Jewish family lived
within 20 miles of Jerusalem, they were required by law to
go Jerusalem for Pentecost, or Feast of Weeks, which marked
the end of the wheat harvest and the beginning of the
Jewish season of "first-fruits." It was celebrated 50 days
after the Passover, hence its name "Pentecost."

LISTENING

The story of Pentecost in Acts (Acts 2:1–21) is a curious one. The disciples are together in a room in Jerusalem and then it is as if they are suddenly outside and there comes the sound of a rushing wind "from the sky." Then another "noise" when fire appears and tongues of fire rest on each one of them.

I am not sure how this sound could be anything but terrifying. I remember very well, as a young man, having to leave a burning building in which I was staying in Central Alberta on the coldest night of the year, and waiting for the fire trucks to arrive. As I stood watching, the sound of rushing wind and of flames incinerating dry wood filled the air and seemed to suck all air toward it. There was a loud whoosh at the beginning, a sound I will never forget. And then some force more powerful than anything I had yet seen in nature was ravaging everything within seconds as I watched.

So I am guessing the sound at Pentecost got everyone's attention, not least the disciples gathered there. In fact, the text says that the sound attracted the attention of devout Jews gathered there from "every nation under heaven," and that the disciples began to speak in the diverse languages of these Jews, who had come to celebrate the Jewish Pentecost or *Shavuot*, the Feast of Weeks.

Listening plays a big part in the story. Listening to wind. Listening to fire. Listening to the sound of one's own language being spoken by a group of Galileans.

Still, it's a difficult story to understand because it's not obvious what is really happening or what it all means. So maybe the easiest way to understand it is to tell the story of its opposite.

A city decided that it wanted to solve the riddle of human misery, the problem of human inferiority. They wanted to answer all unanswered questions once and for all. They were resourceful. They thought they knew how to go about it. So they put all of their resources, all of their brainpower, all the power of their economy, and all of their youth, to work to build the highest building in the world. If they could build a tower as high as God is high, perhaps they could achieve equality with God.

When this tallest of all human buildings was completed, the people processed together to the top, where they celebrated their achievement. When the celebration was over and as they came back down to earth, they found that far from solving their problems the project had raised more questions, caused more hardship, exhausted their young people, and jeopardized their future.

In the end, as they tried to discover who they might be in the era after the tall building, it was as if they all spoke foreign languages to one another; try as they might, they could no longer understand the most simple things spoken by brother to sister, mother to child, life partner to life partner. As a result, the city floundered for generations in its confused collective life. That city was called Babel.

In this story, in contrast to the Pentecost story, you have a sense of people not listening to anything, including each other. Instead, they barge ahead on a whim, on a thought of gaining some kind of advantage or standing that they could not actually, in the end, achieve. Nobody had thought things through.

In the Pentecost story, the use of the natural metaphors of wind and fire, both the sound of wind and the sound and sight of fire, introduce something compelling to the story, so compelling that the writer gets confused as to whether people are inside or outside. Like Moses before them, when he beholds the burning bush in Exodus, they are transfixed. The sight and sound of the elements get people's attention and, in this case, draw them together in a communal experience of kinship. There is not much thinking going on here either, interestingly. The only doing is the talking, the communicating in which everyone seems to understand.

Those in the story and we the reader are being invited into a vision, or what Northrop Frye and his mentor William Blake called the "double vision." What they mean is that in such an experience, in the perceiving of an experience through the human senses – in seeing, hearing, and listening – the participants recognize that they themselves are integral to the experience. It is not just an experience they are perceiving "out there." It is a scene they are experiencing in their totality as human beings. And not only as individuals, but as a collective. We are seeing, hearing, and listening, yes, but we are seeing, hearing and listening together. This is what the strange story of Pentecost is trying to get at.[3]

Here is a different story, a little more like the Pentecost story.[4] In the Middle Ages, the cathedral at Chartres was struck by lightning and burned to the ground. It was a calamity, for Chartres had long been a place of pilgrimage. News of the fire travelled fast. Spontaneously, people came from all over Europe, from all points of the compass. As they gathered among the ruins, slowly and gradually it became clear what they must do. Like the fire and wind spreading through the crowd in Acts 2, a united energy emerged among them and they began to build up the cathedral on its old site.

One story goes that everyone stayed until the building was completed – master builders, workers, artists, clowns, noblemen, priests, burghers. When they were finished, the cathedral they constructed was one of the most beautiful buildings in the world.

Though the details of this story reflect an amalgam of events drawn from a significant span of time, and though some of them have been embellished, to this day the beauty of Chartres Cathedral endures as a testament to what human community can do when love of God, love of neighbour, and love of self, come together. In that sense, the masterpiece that is Chartres is a kind of miracle. It is the "double vision" writ large.

So here we have two stories – of Babel and of Chartres Cathedral – that illustrate something true about human experience. What was the difference between the tower builders at Babel and the cathedral builders of Chartres? In both stories people gather together. At Babel, the people tried to achieve equality with God; they decided they could solve the problem of being God's inferior, and set about to do it. At Chartres, diverse people gathered in response to a human loss. They had no answers, but they waited, they listened. And then, out of the ashes, they built a masterpiece.

Were they all believers when Chartres rose out of the ashes? Is that even important? Were they all believers who experienced the wind and the fire of the spirit at Pentecost? The text does not say. The miracle was that they could communicate despite the fact that they came from all over the known world. That seems to be what the gift of the universal spirit does; it takes down walls that divide us.

Many people think that Pentecost is the birthday of the church. I don't share that view. I think it is the birthday of a time when people of diverse tongues could actually talk to one another about spiritual matters. There was a real listening, a truest kind of hearing. *That* is the miracle.

Frye says that whatever is struck by fire is symbolically the highest point in the world. So maybe the story of Pentecost is the most important revelation, next to the resurrection itself. At Pentecost, the people's heads were on fire with the realization that language is everything, that we need to really listen to one another, and that that kind of communication is the most important thing of all.

If the church or whatever community you put your hopes in does not meet your expectations, think of Chartres. Think of your community not as any institution bent on its own perpetuation. Think of it not as a reservoir of material riches, not as a community intent on convincing people how bad they are, although historically the church has certainly done that. Those things do not represent our "highest" point. All of that is "Babel." Think of Chartres. Think of a listening people gathering to make things better. Together. That's who we really *could* be.

Or think of this story. There is an older man who lives somewhere in the Lower Mainland of British Columbia. I don't know his name. One day he came into my office. He told me a confused story of betrayal and of broken friendship. I just listened. I did nothing. Now, every so often, maybe every six months or so, he calls me. He wants to update me, to tell me more stories. He is still confused, still betrayed; he is more broken still. I listen. I do nothing. And then he thanks me and rings off. That's it. I bet almost every minister in the country could tell you a similar story. When you think of your community at its best, at the highest point in the world, think of that story.

What's Pentecost all about? Well, 40 days after the disciples discovered an empty tomb, people from their known world gathered in Jerusalem, the city Jesus cried over, the city Jesus loved, the city that killed him. Given the circumstances of what had happened earlier, they probably gathered not quite knowing why they were there. They were afraid, perplexed, confused, and yet they gathered. And when they were all together, something unexpected happened. They heard, they saw, they listened, they felt the passion of wind and fire, the miracle of connecting in a meaningful way with other people not necessarily of like mind. Let us listen better. Listen to God. Listen to people. Listen to God-in-people.

Once in a while, we are completely overwhelmed with the passion of wind and fire and we realize that this is what we are about – much more about listening than doing. There is something extraordinary, superlative about this listening. It's about people through whom subtle miracles occur, about people waiting to *give of themselves* in the universal spirit that removes walls and enables miracles to happen.

A PASSIONATE WAITING

For most of my life as a minister, I led occasional services in nursing homes. At first, I wondered at their value.

In my last congregation, we did three such services a month, complete with minister, pianist, and soloist. Depending on the day, I didn't know who in the gathered congregation of people with wheelchairs, walkers, and canes had come of their own free will, or who understood or cared to understand what was happening. People came and went. Some passed through on their way to the smoking room; others stopped by on their way to somewhere else. The staff often chatted amiably in the background. All I really knew, or at least hoped, was that I was delivering a word of consolation to many who were suffering in ways those of us who were younger and well and free could not even begin to imagine. The service was a kind of prayer for them.

But every so often there was a palpable and obvious reward. I noticed the eyes. As the assembled group heard familiar hymns, as they mouthed the words to themselves or joined in broken unison to sing with their fellow residents, I noticed an inner delight. I could see many had recaptured a time when, Sunday after Sunday, they sat in church with friends and lifted their voices together in one glorious melody.

After the service was over, the reward, for me, was the profound and heartfelt gratitude they expressed when I shook their gentle, soft, warm and wrinkled hands. I saw that, by my efforts and a universal spirit besides, life could be a little bit better for a brief while.

It was on one such occasion, during a holy moment of shaking hands after a service, that I became unalterably convinced of the supreme value of these services. As I was shaking hands with her, one woman thanked me for conducting the service entirely in Welsh.

She didn't know, of course, that I belonged to the suspect *English* tribe, and that my spouse and children belonged to the blessedly Welsh. At first, I thought how amused everyone at home would be, and how shocked my in-laws would be, to hear the news that a woman had heard a service spoken in her own language, and their own language, from the likes of me, English to the core. The unlikely and the impossible had been accomplished in this woman's hearing. And then I thought of Pentecost.

It was the 40 days after the resurrection and 50 days after Passover, when Jews from different countries in the known world had gathered in Jerusalem to celebrate Pentecost or *Shavuot*, the Feast of Weeks. But then they were attracted by the passion of wind and fire, and heard a new message of presence among *all* people. What's more, they heard it in their own language from people who did not speak their language. Just like the woman who heard me speaking Welsh.

"In the last days, I will pour out my spirit on all humankind" (Acts 2:17). *All* humankind. Regardless of all barriers and boundaries.

I understood then that the Welsh woman I was shaking hands with had heard something deeply true. Beyond earthly time and space, she had heard the heavenly choir itself. And I had had a part in it. It was a kind of miracle in which I could delight the rest of my days.

These things are so hard to explain. They're especially hard to explain in a world where it's all about "me"; in a world where it's all about the mountaintop experience in the *here and now*; in a world where only the young and the well are considered to have authentic existence; in a world where the idea that a group of old people in a nursing home could feel the passion of wind and fire seems, well, antiquated, quaint, or maybe even a bit creepy.

And of course, it's not just the feeling itself; it's what the feeling *provides*.

For the kindly Welsh woman, it was a profound comfort she took into the coming days. After the Pentecost moment, the populace of the region, and the Romans who occupied it, began to notice strange things happening in their cities. Small pockets of people began to go into the streets to find the sick, to bury bodies rotting outside the city walls, to listen to the babble of people possessed by mistaken spirits, to visit the imprisoned, to feed the hungry. The passion of wind and fire, the sense that the spirit had been poured on all people, pushed the well, the strong, and the able toward action. All people were now blessed. There were no favourites. The world was forced to begin to look with new eyes. It began to listen with new ears.

A SURPRISED AFFECTION

According to the writer of the books of Acts, something strange happened at that "first" Pentecost. The author of Acts struggles with traditional images for the spirit – wind and fire – saying that, without warning, it was as if a wind suddenly started to blow, and that tongues of fire descended on the heads of the disciples, who began to speak in many languages. Soon, the sound drew others from many nations, and everyone understood the disciples, and each other, in their own language, and they were able to talk to each other. In that experience, they were sure they had experienced the divine.

I have a confession to make. I am a servant to scripture. Scripture says something and I pay attention. I need to understand it as best I can so that it can come alive for me. But there are times when the metaphors make me crazy. Fire resting on heads is one of them.

If you have ever read *The New Yorker*, you may remember that sometimes at the end of an article, the magazine placed a little piece called "Block that metaphor," which poked fun at mixed metaphors.

Here's one from a fellow from New York: "I've spent a lot of time in the subways. It's a dark and dank experience. You feel morbid. The environment contributes to fear. The moment that you walk into the bowels of the armpit of the cesspool of crime, you immediately cringe."

Here's another from a senator from Montana: "Until I feel comfortable I'm going to be like a burr under a saddle blanket because I want to know exactly what kind of a pig in a poke we bought here."

And one more from the *LA Times*: "As the vice president arrives in Los Angeles today for a two-day California visit, two distinct Democratic groups are trying to rain on his bandwagon."

The Pentecost story is kind of like that. Fire resting on heads: you have to stretch a bit to get there. I often find the resolution in stories.

A man drops his daughter off at daycare. It is a heart-wrenching experience every single morning. Every parting is like a final parting. Her chin trembles; she blinks hard; her shoulders sag; her body goes limp. She weeps silently as she blows kisses from behind a window pane as he drives away.

Suddenly, the father remembers a much earlier time when he felt that same tug in his gut. It was when he was a teenager and his grandfather died. In that moment, the father began to understand the tearful farewells with his daughter as a small "dying."

But those small absences turned around for him at the end of each day, when he picked his daughter up from daycare. The reunion became a daily miracle. He described it like this. "I hop in the car to return to that home where I left her earlier in the day. What a miracle moment it is. We make eye contact. The morning's shroud buries itself in our reunion, and death's permanent marks are wiped away for a moment ... A complete celebration of life. A huge party, lasting two heartbeats."

What this man describes is a Pentecost moment: the discovery of a phenomenon in which creatures have their own space and share space at the same time.

Or what about this? Two lifelong friends played for opposing hockey teams in the Stanley Cup final. They grew up together in a small town in Nova Scotia. Whenever Colin White and John Sim made contact during the 2000 series, it was news. And they did it a lot. In fact, at times, the hitting got downright fierce. At the end of the last game when one was the winner and one was the loser, the most poignant moment was not when the winner raised the cup above his head. It was the picture of John Sim and Colin White holding each other and weeping. It was a Pentecost moment for the entire world to see.

In her wonderful book *Child's Play*, Canadian Olympian Silken Laumann describes a visit to Laffa, a refugee camp in Sudan on the border with Eritrea. She was visiting with a team of people from the organization Right to Play. The group travelled in white UN vehicles "under the relentless African sun." Paved roads gave way to dirt roads, which gave way to open desert.

"After hours of driving," she writes, "we were able to make out small shadows in the distance that split the sand from the sky. The shadows became tents... rows upon rows of tents lined up by the hundreds, all the same colour as the dust ... And then I saw children, hundreds of them, lingering lethargically beside their mothers, kneeling, standing, motionless. Children with nothing to do."

As Laumann emerged from her vehicle, the crowd of children who had gathered around stepped back. They seemed tentative. They chanted "white man," "white man," in their language. Silken spoke to them in English and they giggled and came closer. "[O]ne brave little girl grasped the index finger of my left hand, and a minute later nine more were holding the rest of my fingers." Laumann writes that, at that point, she had an overwhelming desire to "give them something, to share some part of myself with them."

Laumann began to sing and jump to some skipping songs she remembered from childhood. She writes, "The children pointed...and laughed. Soon I had two hundred children following me around the camp learning ring-around-the-rosy and Marco Polo."

Later, after teaching some girls to play soccer who had never kicked a ball before, Laumann learned that Christian and Muslim girls were playing together for the first time.[5]

Lewis Thomas called that feeling of exultation, that rush of friendship, that spontaneous burst like a fire erupting from the depths, "a surprised affection." I call it something all creatures on earth may discover: Pentecost.

Thomas uncovered it one day when he went to the zoo. He found himself on a deep pathway between two ponds. The ponds were walled with clear glass, so when he stood in the centre of the path he could look into the depths of each pool and see the surface at the same time.

"In one pool, on the right side of the path, was a family of otters; on the other side, a family of beavers," he wrote. So within just a few feet of his face, on opposite sides, beavers and otters were at play, "underwater and on the surface, swimming toward me and then away, more filled with life than any creatures I had ever seen before."

"I was transfixed," he wrote. "[T]here was only one sensation in my head: pure elation mixed with amazement... Swept off my feet, I floated from one side to the other, swivelling my brain, staring astounded at the beavers, then at the otters. I could hear shouts [of] ...wonder ..." He felt a rush of friendship.

And then he says, "[I] learned nothing new about [beavers and otters]. Only about me, and I suspect also about you ... We are stamped with a surprised affection."[6]

I had this experience myself some time ago when I visited the Ripley's Aquarium in Toronto. The aquarium has a room with a moving sidewalk that passes under a massive tank filled with sea creatures: sharks, stingrays, and smaller fish. I was overwhelmed by this sense of kinship. These were fellow creatures. They take a different form than us, but at one time we gathered in the same substance; at some point in the distant past, we humans emerged from the waters of the sea. I too was overcome by a rush of friendship, of surprised affection – like a brush fire of love, swift and consuming, at the highest point in the world.

As the Bible describes Pentecost, it was like a blanket falling from heaven covering a thousand diverse people, gathering them in, making them one. In spite of themselves. In spite of their differences. The Bible says this gift is closely related to the resurrection, the intentional love in the world that surrounds us, which we became more aware of after Jesus' death.

This love is not only there for us to grasp, if we want it. It falls on us naturally, this universal spirit. And we are no longer passive to its accidental occurrence. We want to pursue it, this brush fire of love.

During the summer of 1986 on a 34-hour trip, on a coal-fired train from Hong Kong to Shanghai, my spouse, Sandra, and a seminary classmate of hers met a Chinese woman in their carriage. A man had joined them who spoke English and thus ensued a strange and wonderful conversation.

"What kind of job do you have?" the man and the Chinese woman asked Sandra and her classmate.

"We're ministers in the Christian church," they responded.

Blank faces greeted their pronouncement. "We work for the Christian religion," they tried. "We work in a temple." Still no response.

Suddenly the Chinese woman spotted the simple wooden cross Sandra's friend was wearing and a look of recognition brightened her face.

"Oh! Jesus!" she said and made the sign of the cross.

Sandra and her classmate learned that although the woman was not a Christian herself, her mother had been. Despite the deadly risk of persecution during the time of the Cultural Revolution, her mother had continued to nurture her own faith and had preserved her precious possessions, the objects that helped her keep focused on what she found life-giving: a cross and a Bible. She had stored them in the cold ashes of her fireplace, from where they called forth memories not only of the meaning of the objects, but of the brush fire of love that they kindled.

This brush fire of love, this rush of friendship, this surprised affection – in our complacency, in our freedom to worship (or not) as we please, we can forget how special a gift it is. We can forget how this affection needs to be nurtured forward. It is a good thing to remember, a good thing to recommit ourselves to. In so doing, we embrace the memory of that day when diversity was addressed by wind and fire, when kinship rushed at us, when affection surprised strangers.

NOTES

1.   Frye, *Great Code*, 58.
2.   Frye, *Collected Works*, 33.
3.   Frye, *Double Vision*, 23.
4.   I read this story a long time ago in a brochure introducing the early films of Ingmar Bergman to students at Western University in London, Ontario. The story is attributed to Bergman. Alas the brochure is now lost.
5.   Silken Laumann, *Child's Play: Rediscovering the Joy of Play in Our Families and Communities* (Toronto: Random House, 2006), 210–214.
6.   Lewis Thomas, *Medusa and the Snail: More Notes of a Biology Watcher* (New York: The Viking Press, 1979), 7–11.

CONCLUSION

GOOD FAITH

I N THE PREFACE TO HIS FINAL
BOOK, *The Double Vision*, Northrop Frye seemed a little
nervous that some in the church, in particular his own
church, The United Church of Canada, might find offence in his critical comments about the church as institution. He need not have worried. By July of 1990, he
was so venerated by all that he was beyond criticism.
We had a sense that, in this book, he was writing from
a place high above any single church or denomination.
He was surveying the human landscape and trying to
find the place of the church or, more properly, the
place of Christianity within it.

He also knew, at that point, that he had precious
little time, and where he was going no one could touch
him – literally or figuratively. No one knows, of course,
if he understood that his theological achievement in this
book and in his other theological writings published
after his death come near to the writings of Søren
Kierkegaard in their ability to cut through and find a
faith untainted by church dogma.

In this book, we have found some of the riches in this singular approach to the Bible and Christianity by way of a journey through the church year. Originally, it was a preacher's journey. Then it became a pilgrim's journey. Just as Virgil was Dante's guide through *The Divine Comedy*, Frye has been my guide through the church year. Throughout, we have seen Frye's penetrating vision of a Christianity where the Bible is taken as essential text not *in spite* of its mythological language, but *because* of it. Frye is not interested in finding "the real" story or the "historical" Jesus. To do so is, in his view, to miss what the Bible is all about – myths to live *by* and myths to live *in*. That is, if God is accessible to us at all, God is to be found in the human struggle to live together on this planet. Myths get at that program like no other.

Here Frye the literary critic, together with Frye the believer, finds what is necessary. Living together requires good faith, the kind of love Paul wrote about and which is, according to Frye, the language God must speak – a language of love where between people there is patience and kindness, a refusal to put self above or against the other, where there is no gloating but an enthusiastic pursuit of what is true, and where there is determination to face whatever may come with a confidence.

Just as the beauty in a piece of music may reside in the silence between the notes, so myths of the biblical kind, according to Frye, get at the unseen place where this good faith between people draws forth the realization of human hopes. In this book, we have called this movement the universal spirit.

Even if we cower in the face of fear and sadness, in a commitment to live life together we find that this fear and this sadness is not just our own fear, our own sadness, but a common fear and a common sadness. It is in this realization that we find hope, and it is in this hope, if we persist, that we find a new vision of how society may be.[1]

Notes

1. This is a paraphrase of Frye's statement on Christmas: "The story of Christmas...is in part a story of how [we], by cowering together in a common fear of menace, discovered a new fellowship, in fellowship a new hope, and in hope a new vision of society." Frye, Collected Works, 252.

ACKNOWLEDGEMENTS

I want to thank West Vancouver United Church, my last pastorate, for giving me the time and space to conceive of and bring to fruition the beginnings of this manuscript during a sabbatical they granted me in the spring of 2007. During my time there, as minister, the encouragement and freedom to explore many of these ideas from the pulpit inspired so much of what is written here. Also essential to this inspiration was the music ministry of Gerald Van Wyck, my friend and colleague, who Sunday after Sunday provided, with his excellent choirs and sublime musicianship, a meditative time where all who gathered could find their Christian footing between exquisite notes and silences.

I wish also to thank Dr. Ann Evans, my mentor in ministry and in therapy, who encouraged me to take up the manuscript again and send it to her favourite editor. This I did, very reluctantly. That editor was Mike Schwartzentruber who embraced the idea of a book about Northrop Frye from the beginning, and even through some false starts, continued to believe that this project was worthwhile. In the end it is my book, and Mike helped make it even more so. This is, to my mind, the greatest gift of an editor.

Finally, this book could not have been written without the support of my family. Sandra Severs provided the original editorial comments and stopped me from riding hobby horses off into the sunset. Rhiannon Collett, even as they began their own career as a playwright, encouraged the old man to dream he had a book in him. Last but certainly not least, I thank Bronwyn Collett, who, with her gentle love and caring every single day, continues to make me a better father and a better person to the world.

THE AUTHOR

Don Collett is a Clinical Fellow of the American Association for Marriage and Family Therapy, and a Registered Clinical Counsellor with the British Columbia Association of Clinical Counsellors. He provides therapeutic services to a broad spectrum of individuals, couples, and families from every walk of life and with various mental health concerns. Collett has worked in a wide range of mental health settings including employment centres and First United Church in the Downtown Eastside of Vancouver. Currently, he is under contract to provide therapeutic assistance to employees of Vancouver Coastal Health. As a minister with the United Church of Canada for over 35 year years, Collett brings his faith and theology to these various contexts when it is appropriate. He conducts workshops on various mental health issues and now specializes in addressing the particular challenges front line municipal workers face when encountering mental health issues in the community. He is the current President of the BC Association for Marriage and Family Therapy and sits on the Board of the Canadian Association for Marriage and Family Therapy. This is his first book.

Author photo: Rhiannon Collett

REVELATION
FOR PROGRESSIVE CHRISTIANS
A Seven Session Study Guide

Donald Schmidt

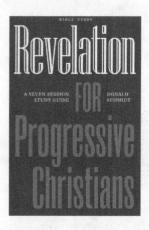

More material has probably been written about the biblical book of Revelation than the rest of the Bible combined – or at least it can seem that way. What's more, people who write or talk about Revelation often have a passion that defies all logic. They speak vividly and forcefully about plagues, and judgements, and the end of the world. All interesting themes – but are they the real concern or message of Revelation?

Revelation for Progressive Christians is a seven-session study guide that invites readers to explore Revelation as a fun, hope-filled book that contains a lot of fanciful imagery and symbolic references, to be sure, but that, at its core, offers words of assurance and hope to the church and its people today.

ISBN 978-1-77343-150-5
5.5" x 8" | 100 pp | paperback | $14.95

WOOD LAKE

IMAGINING, LIVING, AND TELLING
THE FAITH STORY.

Wood Lake is the faith story company.

It has told
- the story of the seasons of the earth, the people of God, and the place and purpose of faith in the world;
- the story of the faith journey, from birth to death;
- the story of Jesus and the churches that carry his message.

Wood Lake has been telling stories for more than 35 years. During that time, it has given form and substance to the words, songs, pictures, and ideas of hundreds of storytellers.

Those stories have taken a multitude of forms – parables, poems, drawings, prayers, epiphanies, songs, books, paintings, hymns, curricula – all driven by a common mission of serving those on the faith journey.

WOOD LAKE PUBLISHING INC.
485 Beaver Lake Road
Kelowna, BC, Canada V4V 1S5
250.766.2778

www.woodlake.com